SMITH & DELI-CIOUS

FOOD FROM OUR DELI
(THAT HAPPENS TO BE VEGAN)

SHANNON MARTINEZ & MO WYSE

Hardie Grant

BOOKS

FRESH
SALADS 035

SUPER YUM
Sweet Case 143

HEARTY 057
SOUPS

Simple
PASTRY &
DOUGH 181

DELICIOUS
Ready
085 –meals

189 EASY
BASICS

PIE
MOREISH 131
FILLINGS

TASTY 213
DRINKS

Smith & Deli is a feeling more than a place.

Our Deli was born out of necessity. 1. We had outgrown our restaurant. And 2. Shannon was going creatively stir crazy (but we'll come back to that).

We had outgrown Smith & Daughters, our plant-based Latin restaurant on Brunswick Street in Fitzroy, Melbourne. We knew we needed a bigger space and we needed it yesterday. Less than a year after opening the restaurant, we were toasting all our current staff (who didn't know what they were getting into) and the signing of the lease on Smith & Deli. However, it was a much, much more ambitious build. The restaurant had previously functioned as a restaurant, while the Deli was an IT office, complete with a meeting room and a floor of open-plan cubicles. Everything had to go. Transformation is an understatement.

Running a shop is so different from running a restaurant, especially when you commit to a made-to-order sandwich bar with thirty-two varieties, rotating sweets, salads, dips, pies, sausage rolls, scrolls, pizzas, ready-meals, cheeses, meats and groceries. We had a booming trade, queues around the block and an ever-changing landscape of problem-solving to get our space sorted. And then, just like that, the place became more than a place; we had created a community. We created somewhere for people to come every day, on their way to work, on their lunch breaks, while walking their dog. We became their Saturday place and their happy place. The park next to the Deli became unofficially known as Smith & Park, where on any given day our signature bandana-print sandwich paper can be spotted at picnics across the lawn.

Our 'Eat Vegan' iron sign out the front has been affectionately called the Leaning Tower of Veganism. If you didn't take a photo of it, did you really go? And we are a destination spot for food lovers and vegans across the world. How did this happen? We like to think it was born out of hard work and innovation, creating the first vegan deli in the world, making sure our products are always good, and creating the best customer service team to match. We're committed to creating so much more than a meal – it's an experience.

This is what we want to translate for you in this book. We want you to feel the sentiments we hear daily: that people are in heaven, or feel at home, or they can't believe they're eating something they haven't had in ten years. We want you to feel the warmth of our team and the care they put into every pie and every tiny hand-cut potato; there's so much love in every single bite. We have customers that, to this day, say their partners have no idea they're eating vegan food, and that's definitely still one of our favourite compliments. Others say that our sausage rolls convinced someone in their life that vegan food isn't complete garbage. It's all about changing minds and empowering our staff and customers.

The other reason we created the Deli was to give Shannon a place to create something new every single day. Smith & Daughters' small kitchen, along with a menu that only changed seasonally, made it impossible for Shannon to try new things and challenge herself. Now, Shannon refers to the Deli as her little science lab: her place to play. The Deli has changed everything for her. It has given her the freedom to make exciting things happen all the time, and there are new victories daily. She even gets to talk about how to mimic blood when she's creating the world's best burgers or sausages. And she is still committed to making dishes that create food memories and make people emotional: those dishes that are purely for the people. Our goal

is to expand, always; to show people that vegan food has moved beyond the trend, the joke or the dirty word it once was, and to get in the faces of the naysayers.

The Deli is also the place where no one has to think. If you're vegan, we've done the work for you. Finally, a corner store where you can pick up your basics as well as a ready-meal and have no doubts. Meat eaters have that luxury; they can go into any shop and get anything they want. Our Deli, like the recipes in this book, provides a place where any vegan can go and be spoiled for choice, and we can look after them. It's a comfortable food haven and, most importantly, it's convenient.

One of the roadblocks to vegan cooking is efficiency and convenience. You can't just go and grab a jar or box of something and, if you're making a meal, it's often a lengthy, all-day process. This book aims to stop all this nonsense. We've given you basic staples: doughs, pastries and sauces to keep in the fridge so you can set yourself up to make meals in about twenty minutes. Cook smart, not hard.

We wish all of you readers could take a stroll in our tiny store, be greeted by our effervescent staff, pat a cute dog and gaze at the dozens of rotating sweets, meals and salads in our cases. But we know that's impossible, so we created this book. Our goal is to connect with as many people as possible and show them that vegan food is so much more than what they think, and this is it. This is for you.

There's one thing, and one thing only, that stops the Deli from operating: dogs. When there's a dog in the shop, all the staff are out the front causing a scene, oohing and aahing and patting and taking photos. Sorry, customers, there will be a brief interruption in your service; there's a dog in the shop.

(Oh, and we serve puppacinos for those hounds who brave the lines.)

LENNY

EVIE

SUGAR

ANOUSHKA

SHEEBA

THEO

Staff

We know we're the most fortunate business owners in the world, and it all comes down to the solid-gold-in-human-form we employ. We truly have the best staff in the world: people who are genuine, warm, fun to be around, hardworking and simply incredible.

Lara (epitome of relentless love) is our front of house manager. Her enthusiasm and excitement is incomparable. Sandwich press broken? There's an hour wait in line? You instantly feel better with one short Lara announcement: words that feel like a hug from your best friend. When asked what the Deli means to her, Lara said, 'It means working with some of the greatest people I've ever met. It means making up songs about inanimate objects, it means laughing until my belly hurts. It means dancing every day, it means working our guts out every day and still smiling at the end of it, ready to do it all again.' And she does.

All good managers need their support. The team is brilliant, but there's one soul most across it all – our assistant manager, Emma. Rain or shine, she is there for us, she ensures the shop runs without flaws, is stocked to the gills, and is perfectly perfect. She's the Timon as Lara is the Pumba. We may all have PMA (positive mental attitude) but they have what you call HMA: hakuna matata attitude. We couldn't do it without them.

We nurture our staff and our relationships, and are extremely fortunate to have a lot of the original crew. But our management team and diehards are the ones keeping our Deli ship afloat. We know we couldn't grow this business if it weren't for these amazing humans. They're the people who fill in the gaps of our weaknesses, the ones who create that special experience for customers, and who come up with new flavours of everything every day.

When we asked our pastry manager, El, about working at the Deli, she replied, 'I get to work with a team of people who are so invested, genuine and wholehearted in their job. It's a place that could never be replicated.'

The Deli could never be replicated because of these precious souls right here. These are the people making this world a better place. Thanks, team.

LARA MIHAN

Manager

Question most asked by customers
Is everything vegan? Really?
Are you hiring?

What the Deli means to you
It reminds me that together we can make great things
happen in this world – without harming anyone.

Favourite non-food thing at the Deli
Staff.

Favourite non-Deli activity
Hanging with my husband and dog. And gardening.

Dogs or cats
DOGS! All the dogs, please.

EL ROSA

Pastry Manager

Question most asked by customers
Is this gluten-free?

What the Deli means to you
I'm a baby in this industry and I have total freedom to
explore and improve my skills daily. Shannon's knowledge
and mentorship is such an incredible gift.

Favourite non-food thing at the Deli
Coffee. Ha ha. Good Lord, the coffee.

Favourite non-Deli activity
My hobby is my profession. I come home and keep baking,
cooking, experimenting and eating. I'm damn lucky, I know.

Dogs or cats
Cats. Duh. Siouxsie and Stevie are my babies.

JACQUELINE SANSONETTI

Drinks Manager

Question most asked by customers
What's your favourite?!

Favourite customer story
When we were running the *Twin Peaks* drink specials, a few people gifted the Deli some really amazing *Twin Peaks* artworks. We really do get in the best!

Favourite non-food thing at the Deli
People!

Dogs or cats
'Dogs AND cats', right?! Cuz I've got enough love for them both!

EMMA JAMES

Assistant Manager

Question most asked by customers
Is everything vegan?!? Are you sure??????

Favourite non-food thing at the Deli
Lara.

Favourite non-Deli activity
Listening to true crime podcasts and playing pinball.

Dogs or cats
Both. (I'm assuming this is a trick question!)

Customers

There will never be a more dedicated bunch of people. Since day one, our customers have been with us: they did a dance as we opened our doors, and have gotten drenched as they lined up in the rain. We have hundreds of regulars and they all are known by name, as are their coffee orders, their dietary requirements, their favourite food and their dogs' names. We are just as much a fan of them as they are of us. We mutually brighten each other's days; when they skip a day, we take notice and, if one of our team is sick, they notice. We have a customer we'd like to single out who posted – after a long wait in line on a public holiday – 'I just go to @smithanddeli for all the positivity and smiles tbh. I would probably have thrown down $30 weekly for that without the food.'

We have heard about the cult following of some of our products, and we know the planes people catch and the lengths Uber drivers go to for out-of-town guests. Our customers are some of the craziest, most faithful people we've ever met – even if they've only been once. We know we've changed their lives, we know we've blown their minds (and diets and wallets), but their emotional impact on us is just as great.

THE DELI IS SO MUCH MORE THAN A SHOP. IT'S A COMMUNITY THAT WE'VE CREATED TOGETHER AND, FOR THAT, WE'RE FOREVER GRATEFUL.

Shannon (still) isn't vegan

An update on the explanation in our first book of how a non-vegan could be so invested in making plant-based meals: no, Shannon still isn't vegan, and yes, she's still making ground-breaking discoveries for plant-based substitutions.

There's something so invasive when online criticisms are (STILL!) flung in our direction, questioning our ethics, our reason for being and how we could possibly be making a difference. My personal MO is to not read the comments, to put my head down and continue fighting the good fight – but I'll tell you, it gets mighty old when I have to defend my business to people who should be on our side. Why oh why do vegans criticise a vegan business? Especially one that reaches so many people and is doing far more for veganism than many other businesses?

People are attracted to a plant-based way of eating for many reasons, and we needn't all share the same perspective. If there's someone out there who genuinely cares about innovation and wants to create dishes that don't use animal flesh, that's exciting! Purely from a sentimental point of view, if someone is driven to make food that replicates your favourite childhood dishes – the ones you thought you'd never eat again after going vegan – that's someone I want cooking. That's someone who will change the way the world thinks about food. That person is Shannon.

Even though I'm vegan myself, there is no one I'd rather share this business with than my meat-eating business partner. She's the most creative, innovative, driven and focused chef in this industry, with the bonus that she strives to create more, do better and change the way the world eats. She's also convinced some serious meat eaters to go vegan, or at least change their perspectives on veganism. Look at all the chefs in her community who have increased the vegan options on their menus because of her influence. Let us focus on adding things back into our food rather than taking them out – on making food taste the way it should.

Shannon never shies away from a challenge. She is her hardest critic, and if something isn't good enough it doesn't go on our shelves. She always aims to shut down the notion that vegan food is just 'good enough'; there's no 'good enough' when it comes to Shannon. It has to be the best. If that's not the highest level of commitment, then I don't know what is.

How to use this book

Following the recipes

It's not as basic as pick the prettiest picture, get the ingredients and follow the method. No way! We want to lay down some ground rules, the first is that we want this to be a good experience for you; one that keeps you coming back. We hope we've given you newbie vegan cooks (or newbie cooks in general) enough guidance so you're not going mad with the lack of instruction, but those experienced cooks enough of a framework. Basically, don't follow the rules. Get loose with it. If you don't have some of the stuff, that's fine – just go with it – even for recipes that do call for specific veg, just substitute! Use more spice, or make it saltier! Your call. This won't impact anything but YOUR enjoyment of the dish. We don't endorse you following recipes to the letter because their creator, Shannon herself, doesn't follow recipes. Use them as a guide, as inspiration. But when it comes to pastry, if you're not an accomplished baker, then follow the recipes for real. BUT if you are a baker or an accomplished pastry chef, make it Shannon's way first then mess around with the recipe. Take it and have a play. Get the general feel, then go nuts.

Chicken stock

PLEASE. WE BEG YOU. DON'T THROW AWAY THE BOOK BECAUSE A RECIPE LISTS CHICKEN STOCK! You think that's funny? Well, we wish we did too. But this really happened – multiple times – with our first book. There were people who a) skipped reading this very substitutions section in the first book and b) couldn't get past the fact that we weren't going to put the word 'vegan' before every instance of butter, milk, chicken, etc. THIS IS A VEGAN BOOK, SO WE'RE REFERRING TO THE VEGAN VERSIONS OF THESE PRODUCTS.

They exist. Some of them exist at your mainstream grocery store and are already vegan, without advertising as such. They just don't contain animal ingredients. The number of times we had to send a photo of our chicken stock to readers so they wouldn't throw out the book was comical, especially when the vegan craze caught on to this mainstream stock supplier. This particular product now markets itself with the tagline 'suitable for vegans', where once it only used terms like 'cholesterol-free', 'gluten-free' and 'healthy'. Lighten up, people.

Fake meat

Regarding the use of mock meats: we know there are some real pros and cons when it comes to a book calling for fake meats, the major con being accessibility. We have included mutton chunks, faux bacon, sausage, chicken and prawns, etc., but don't let this turn you off; it really doesn't limit you in any way. As with everything else, please use what's available to you. Use your favourite brands of mock meats and, if you hate mock meat or can't get your hands on it, don't use it!

Shannon can, has, and will continue to make her own fake meat, but it's tricky, time consuming and often hard to nail, even for an accomplished chef. There are plenty of products out there doing the job. So, for this book, and the ease of making these recipes, use the mock products on the shelves at your local shop. The key is to make good-tasting food because you have a fond memory of it and it needs to be recreated. We haven't included fake meat in this book just for the sake of it. That said, not all dishes need fake meat (some are just better off being purely veg), but some do, and in these cases we have done it properly. Trust us. We're not just throwing mayo on some chickpeas and calling it tuna salad. Enough of that.

Beef ... an ode to mutton chunks

With all the mock meats Shannon has used in the past fifteen years – and you name it, she's tried it, imported, smuggled and wired it – we've come a very long way. The first ones we used were Asian mock meats and, as Shannon puts it (nicely), they were simply average. The most realistic product she has cooked with is mutton chunks. They're made purely of dried, compressed mushrooms, with no thickeners or gums. They're tasty and don't weigh down your stomach and make you feel like crap. The mutton chunks have the texture of slow-braised beef or lamb, except you don't have to wait five hours to eat them.

Important basics

1. Don't rush. Don't crowd the pan. Layer your ingredients and let them do their thing. We know you can go rogue and do what you want, but when you put everything in a pan at a high temperature, you're just steaming; you lose the flavours and complexities of the food, which so often happens with dishes like tofu scrambles and stir-fries. Let's break this steamy habit.

2. Always use the best ingredients you can buy, even – especially – the simple stuff. Use nice extra-virgin olive oil and the best local sea salt flakes: whatever you can get your hands on, just don't use the crappy iodised table stuff. And freshly ground pepper: always grind your pepper; never ever use the boxed stuff. If you have to, grind up your pepper in advance and use it throughout the week.

3. Sometimes recipes call for salt or pepper. Follow that, but definitely add more salt and pepper if you wish. It's such a personal thing. We like our food salty, but some people don't.

4. Same goes for oils and fats. If you're someone who likes to use smaller amounts of fats and oils, feel free to reduce, but please don't expect it to taste like food from our Deli. It will still be tasty, but it won't be the same. As we all know, restaurant food tastes good because of the oil and other good stuff we try to reduce in our home cooking. Simply put, we always encourage people to experiment, but if you want the food to have maximum flavour, you're best off following the recipe.

5. Fresh herbs are the only herbs. Shannon means it when she says it. Don't use dried herbs if you can help it, especially as so many mock meats already overuse dried herbs. The only exception to this rule is oregano. Even if you don't usually cook with fresh herbs, we suggest you try it, or blend them with oil and freeze in ice-cube trays so at least you have fresh frozen herbs; they're way better than dried. And even if you have a black thumb, try growing some herbs yourself, even if you live in a tiny apartment. Your food will be better for it.

6. Cooking times. Now this may throw you off, especially if you're a rules follower. We don't often state how long to cook things in exact minutes. We prefer to give you a colour or a texture to look for as a guide. No two ovens or stoves are the same, and we don't all cook with gas or industrial ovens. We'd love you to learn your kitchen and know how your appliances work. Does your oven run hot or cold? Do you know your pots and pans? If you know your kitchen and you know how your equipment works, your instincts will be more reliable.

7. Portions. Go big and stay home (on your couch, and eat all of it). Why make small portions when leftovers are the best? With most recipes, except for pastry, we have to tell you we are aiming big. We've assumed that you're healthy eaters, like us, so most recipes serve four to six people. Keep in mind, we make food like we're preparing for the end of days, but this is not a rule of thumb; we don't know how much you like to eat.

8. Sections of this book. Keep the basics and doughs in your fridge/freezer at all times – it will make your life better and make using this book easier. Having soup in the freezer is like having pain medication on hand; you never know when you'll need it. When it comes to salads, play with the veg and keep the dressings the same. Make what you like. We hate restaurants that cover every continent of the world in the entrée section. Africa, Italy and Germany all before you've even looked at the mains? It doesn't work, but we get away with it because we're a deli servicing the needs of people who don't want to eat the same thing every day. We want variety, please!

9. Feel free to freestyle these recipes. Many of the ready-meals can also double as pie fillings and, whenever you make dough, be sure to make heaps of it so you can prep for multiple meals at a time. Fill up some pies and freeze them, or use leftover pie filling as a pizza topping, or serve it over pasta or rice. So much versatility.

10. This book uses 20 ml (¾ fl oz) tablespoons; cooks using 15 ml (½ fl oz) tablespoons should be generous with their tablespoon measurements. Metric cup measurements are used, i.e. 250 ml (8½ fl oz) for 1 cup; in the US a cup is 237 ml (8 fl oz), so American cooks should be generous with their cup measurements; in the UK, a cup is 284 ml (9½ fl oz), so British cooks should be scant with their cup measurements.

11. Oven temperatures are for fan-forced ovens; if you have a conventional oven, increase the temperature by 20°C (35°F).

Equipment

You've invested in the book. You've invested in the ingredients. You're off to a good start; now it's time to get the goods. Invest in some quality cookware and utensils, especially knives – the good stuff that will last forever. It will make cooking even more enjoyable, and it's better than cutting yourself trying to use a cheap, blunt knife.

Confidence

Same as our first book: don't be scared in the kitchen. Enjoy the process and make time for food. We've put the work into these recipes and chosen some of our favourites, so now's the time to impress that shit-talking uncle with a crazy good beef bourguignon. Now's the time to take doughnuts to the office and convince everyone you don't just eat grass. Now's the time to stock your fridge with easy-to-make staples that don't come in plastic packets. It's time to gain confidence in the kitchen and in your dietary choices. Vegan food is good, especially when it's made by someone who knows what they're doing. With this book, we hope to empower you to produce the same quality of food that makes non-vegans tell us daily they'd go vegan. Break out the pots and pans and get cooking, friend!

Substitutions

Heads up, this is a VEGAN cookbook. When we use words like milk, butter and meat, we're referring to substitutes. Not all milks, butters and meats come from animals, and the ones we use only come from plants. Here are a few of our favourites:

Beef Whatever brand of vegan meat replacement you can get, use it. Anything resembling a chunk of beef. Shannon's favourite is mutton chunks made from mushrooms, which are available at Asian grocers.

Belacan (see Kimchi, pages 190–1) You can find vegan versions of this amazing shrimp paste in Asian grocery stores or online.

Black salt Again, go to the effort to find it in your local Indian grocer or health food store – though, hot tip: the Indian grocer will sell it at a tenth of the price. We don't mean literally black salt, we mean the sulphuric stuff that comes from the natural mines in India, Pakistan, Nepal and the Himalayan ranges. This is what makes 'not eggs' taste like eggs, and it mimics the taste of eggs like nothing else, except eggs themselves. You're going to want it for that Egg Salad (page 127).

Butter Nuttelex, but any dairy-free margarine can work.

Cheese Green Vie makes tasty vegan cheese (in different varieties) that is readily available in mainstream grocery stores. You can also search out a coconut-based cheese. However, any vegan cheese should do the trick for the recipes that call for it. By now you will have found your favourite, so just use whichever one you like the most. That said, choose the cheese that makes the most sense for the recipe you're making. If you want a true cheesy flavour, opt for something stronger than mild mozzarella.

Chicken Again, there are so many chicken alternatives available in mainstream supermarket fridges and frozen sections. Even since publishing our first book, many more alternatives have become available. Just have a look. A word of caution, though. If you're mock-meat shopping in an Asian grocery store (which is super fun), beware of mock meats that are too heavily spiced or overpowering, as they aren't always right for the recipe you're making. That is, unless you're making an Asian-style dish, of course.

Eggs No Egg or Egg Replacer. No Egg just happens to be something we can readily get our hands on in Australia at most natural food stores. Search out the newest, hottest not-an-egg product in your area; there are heaps coming out.

Fish sauce Yes, you can go without it in most recipes, but it won't be as good. Go to the effort to try to find it in your local Asian market or health food store. There are brands that produce amazing versions – simply ask your local shop to stock it.

Milk Our preference is a malt-free, non-GMO soy, but use whatever you can get your hands on. You can also use other types of milks, especially when baking, but avoid sweetened or flavoured milks, as these can alter the final product quite a bit.

Nutritional yeast Available at all health food stores.

Parmesan Track down Green Vie parmesan and your life will be changed forever. In Shannon's opinion (at the release of this book), it has the cheesiest flavour – with that natural umami taste – of all the vegan cheeses.

Sausage There are so many veggie sausages out there now, just pick your brand; everyone has their favourite. Try to match the flavour of the sausage to the flavour of the recipe you're making.

Sour cream & cream cheese Tofutti still reigns supreme. However, there are a lot more exciting cream cheese alternatives coming out, particularly in America and Europe. Tofutti is the best we can get our hands on here in Australia, but keep your eyes peeled.

Stock Some supermarkets carry vegan chicken and beef stock. Check the labels in the mainstream stock and health food sections. You'll find some stocks are vegan anyway without technically being labelled as 'vegan products'. But you can ALWAYS just use veg stock for these recipes, even if the recipe says otherwise.

TVP, or Textured Vegetable Protein, which you can find in health food stores. It's definitely worth getting, is cost-effective and great for recipes that call for longer cooking, i.e. chilli or bolognese (though Shannon's preference is veggie mince, if you can find it).

Wine Kind of a funny one, we know, but not all wine is vegan. Most are filtered through fish scales or milk products. Get online, have a read and pick your favourite. Shannon's advice re. cooking with wine is that if you wouldn't drink it, you shouldn't cook with it. AND if you don't drink and need it for cooking, simply freeze your leftover wine in cup measures in resealable plastic bags.

Worcestershire Though traditionally made with anchovies, store-brand worcestershire sauce is often vegan by accident. A lot of the newer products use tamarind instead of anchovy. Our advice: use the cheaper brands and steer clear of old-school ones.

FRESH
SALADS

Not all salads are created equal. Ours are the kind you make friends with! Most are mega meal-sized salads that will knock your socks off with flavour and their ability to fill you up. These salads are so versatile, and we strongly encourage everyone to use their favourite veg. Just because we give a list of veg, it doesn't mean you can't have a play using whatever you like. We recommend keeping the dressings the same, but if there's an ingredient you don't like, replace it. This chapter reveals some of the finest Deli salads, so get to it and enjoy!

Pickled Chinese Mushrooms

Serves 4–6 as a side salad

Here's the recipe where we get to talk about Shannon's favourite food in the whole world: Sichuan. There's nothing quite like the sting, spice and numbness of Sichuan cuisine. One day, she will be adopted by a granny in the Sichuan province and we'll lose her forever. Until then, she can eat all the Sichuan food in Melbourne and make it for herself at home. Starting with this amazing pickled mushroom salad. Yeah, it's pickled mushroom, but it's meant to be eaten like a salad.

'Unusual' is definitely the word. It's rubbery, it's crunchy, it's sharp, and boy is it spicy. If these aren't your textures and flavours, you may hate this dish. But for those of you who like the sound of it, make it, store it in the fridge and know that it gets better with time.

INGREDIENTS

30 g (1 oz) dried shiitake mushrooms, sliced

15 g (½ oz) dried wood ear mushrooms

½ carrot, sliced into discs

2 teaspoons salt

3 teaspoons sesame oil

4 teaspoons soy sauce

4 teaspoons rice vinegar

4 teaspoons black vinegar

2 teaspoons caster (superfine) sugar

1 teaspoon sesame seeds, toasted

4 thin slices of ginger, julienned

1 small garlic clove, minced (approx. ½ teaspoon)

1 red chilli, with seeds, sliced

2 teaspoons Sichuan crispy chilli oil (optional)

small handful of coriander (cilantro), including stems, chopped

¼ red onion, thinly sliced

Put the mushrooms in a saucepan and cover with cold water. Bring to the boil, then simmer over a low heat for 5 minutes, adding the carrot during the last minute of cooking time. Drain and refresh under cold water.

Mix the remaining ingredients in a large bowl and stir until the sugar and salt have dissolved. Add the mushrooms and carrots to the pickling liquid and stir to coat. Leave to sit for at least 30 minutes, stirring often.

Beetroot, Lentil, Yoghurt & Dill

Serves 4–6 as a side salad

One thing we love at Smith & Deli is dispelling salad myths. We agree, you don't always make friends with salad. But when you get a meatier, more filling salad – one that can be eaten as a meal – you have a winner. Lentil and beetroot is a classic combo, and all these delicious Middle Eastern flavours are just meant to be together. Perfect as a large, hearty salad to bring to any occasion.

INGREDIENTS

500 g (1 lb 2 oz) baby beetroot (or large beetroot, which will need to be cooked longer. P.S. Mixed colours are nice)

185 g (6½ oz/1 cup) dried puy lentils or black lentils, cooked

750 ml (25½ fl oz/3 cups) water

1 bay leaf

handful of dill, roughly torn

small handful of mint, leaves picked and shredded

large handful of rocket (arugula)

large handful of sorrel leaves (optional)

30 g (1 oz/⅓ cup) flaked almonds, toasted

S&P

Dressing

125 g (4½ oz/½ cup) natural yoghurt (not vanilla, not sweetened)

2 tablespoons lemon juice (approx. 1 lemon)

2 tablespoons olive oil

1 teaspoon salt

pepper, to taste

1 teaspoon dukkah spice mix or Middle Eastern spice mix (if you can't get your hands on that, 1 teaspoon cumin will do), plus extra to garnish

Prepare your beetroot first. Put them in a large pot, cover with water and bring to the boil. Reduce the heat and simmer for 40 minutes. Drain and leave to cool.

If you have used different-coloured beetroot, either boil them separately or place each colour on a piece of foil, drizzle with a little oil, wrap and bake at 180°C (350°F) for 30 minutes to 1 hour until a sharp knife easily pierces the beetroot. Remove from the oven and set aside until cool enough to handle.

Put the lentils in a large saucepan with the water and bay leaf. Bring to the boil, then reduce the heat and simmer for 20–25 minutes, or until just cooked. Be sure to not overcook the lentils, as you want them to be slightly firm in the salad. Drain and run them under cold water to stop the cooking process. Discard the bay leaf.

Using your hands, rub the beetroot to remove their skins. (You can wear gloves for this if you like – but if you don't, be prepared to have pink hands for the rest of the day.) If you like, you can leave any stalks on; they're totally edible and look really nice. Depending on the size of your beetroot, halve or quarter them. (Shannon prefers a combo of sizes to give the salad a bit of texture.)

Mix the lentils, beetroot, herbs, rocket, sorrel and almonds together in a bowl and season to taste.

To make the dressing, combine all the ingredients in a bowl.

When you're ready to serve, either use the dressing to coat the salad evenly, or spread the dressing on a serving dish and pile the salad on top. A heads up: if you toss the dressing through the salad, everything turns a bit pink. Garnish with a little extra dukkah.

Barley, Feta, Zucchini, Mint & Lemon

Serves 4–6 as a side salad

When zucchini is prepared well, there's nothing like it. This is a fully delicious, hearty salad featuring zucchini you could eat like candy once it's been marinated and chargrilled. It's also one that gets better the longer you leave the flavours to develop, so allow it to sit for about an hour before eating. The barley and zucchini will surprise you with the amount of flavour they take on and, bonus, this salad keeps well in the fridge. Make a big batch for a party, or to have around for delicious side salads.

INGREDIENTS

220 g (8 oz/1 cup) pearled barley

1 litre (34 fl oz/4 cups) water

150 g (5½ oz/1 cup) Feta (page 197)

large handful of picked flat-leaf (Italian) parsley leaves

large handful of picked mint leaves

¼ red onion, thinly sliced

50 g (1¾ oz/⅓ cup) toasted pepitas (pumpkin seeds), to serve

85 g (3 oz/½ cup) pitted green olives, to serve

Zucchini Marinade

1 large garlic clove, minced

zest of 1 lemon

½ teaspoon salt

½ teaspoon dried oregano

generous pinch of pepper

½ teaspoon chilli flakes

¼ teaspoon cumin seeds

60 ml (2 fl oz/¼ cup) extra-virgin olive oil

2 large zucchini (courgettes) (mixed varieties if available), ends removed, halved lengthways, cut into 1 cm (½ in) dice

Dressing

2 tablespoons lemon juice (approx. 1 lemon)

1 teaspoon dijon mustard

½ teaspoon salt

pepper, to taste

1 teaspoon agave syrup or ½ teaspoon caster (superfine) sugar

80 ml (2½ fl oz/⅓ cup) extra-virgin olive oil

Combine the barley and water in a large saucepan and bring to the boil, then reduce the heat and simmer over a low heat for 40 minutes, or until just cooked. Be sure to not overcook the barley, as you want it to be firm in the salad. (We're not making soup here, people.) Drain and set aside.

While your barley is cooking, mix all the zucchini marinade ingredients, except the zucchini, together in a bowl. Add the zucchini and mix with your hands until well coated. Heat a chargrill pan over a high heat and grill the zucchini until nice char lines appear.

Combine the cooked barley and grilled zucchini in a bowl, then add the feta, parsley, mint and onion.

To make your dressing, whisk together all the ingredients, except the olive oil, in a small bowl. Slowly drizzle in the oil while whisking to emulsify the dressing. Pour the dressing over the salad and mix well. Toss through the toasted pepitas and olives to serve.

Photo page 102.

Creamy Pesto Potato

Serves 4–6 as a side salad

It's like clockwork: if it's Saturday at the Deli, you're eating potato salad. Not sure when or why this happened, but we know that if we didn't have potato salad on a Saturday our customers would probably fire us.

Lucky for you, you've been a smart cook and already have pesto and mayo all ready to go in your fridge or freezer. After that, cooking the potatoes is the only effort required with our picnic winner. Creamy pesto just makes sense, and with the green of the pesto and the rocket, you can actually fool yourself into thinking you're eating a salad, not just creamy potatoes.

INGREDIENTS

1 kg (2 lb 3 oz) chat (new) potatoes (but you can use any variety)

1 tablespoon salt, plus extra to taste

60 g (2 oz/¼ cup) Pesto (page 201)

250 g (9 oz/1 cup) Mayonnaise (page 200)

2 tablespoons red-wine vinegar

250 g (9 oz) cherry tomatoes, halved

½ red onion, thinly sliced

2 handfuls of rocket (arugula)

S&P

Put the potatoes in a large saucepan and cover with cold water. Add the salt and bring to the boil, then reduce the heat to medium and simmer until the potatoes are just soft when pierced with a sharp knife. Drain and rinse under cold running water, then set aside.

Make a dressing by mixing the pesto, mayonnaise and red-wine vinegar in a bowl. Set aside.

Halve or quarter the potatoes, depending on how you like them, and combine with the cherry tomatoes, onion and rocket in a salad bowl. Add the dressing, toss to coat and season with salt and pepper.

Photo page 103.

Ze German Potato

Serves 4–6

My reverence for potato salad is felt most strongly when it comes to Ze German. Call me a sucker for pickled ingredients, but sauerkraut AND pickles AND wholegrain mustard, all with potatoes? I'm done for. We knew the bacon would reel most people in. I mean, bacon and potatoes: no-brainer. People love a German potato salad experience. You'll see.

INGREDIENTS

1 kg (2 lb 3 oz) chat (new) potatoes (but you can use any variety)

1 tablespoon salt, plus extra to taste

150 g (5½ oz/1 cup) sauerkraut, chopped

6 bacon rashers (slices), diced and cooked

2 tablespoons extra-virgin olive oil

145 g (5 oz/½ cup) dill pickles, chopped

2 celery stalks, finely diced

½ brown onion, finely diced

large handful of dill, chopped

pepper, to taste

Dressing

250 g (9 oz/1 cup) Mayonnaise (page 200)

2 tablespoons wholegrain mustard

1 tablespoon apple-cider vinegar

3 tablespoons dill pickle juice

Put the potatoes in a large saucepan and cover with cold water. Add the salt and bring to the boil, then reduce the heat to medium and simmer until the potatoes are just soft when pierced with a sharp knife. Drain and rinse under cold running water, then set aside.

To make the dressing, combine all the ingredients in a bowl and set aside.

Halve or quarter the potatoes depending on how you like them. Combine with the remaining ingredients in a salad bowl, add the dressing and toss to coat. Season well.

Greek Watermelon

Serves 4–6 as a side salad

Sure, you can find Greek salads everywhere. But there's one catch. Though they are usually vegetarian, they are rarely ever vegan. And scraping feta off cucumbers, olives and, particularly, watermelon is no easy task. In fact, it is usually always an abandoned mission. As often as they tell you, 'It's just a bit of cheese', that little bit is still cheese, buddy!

Sidenote: this is definitely a dish we have to attach a 'hands off, staff' note to, otherwise the bowl goes out a lot emptier than it ought to.

INGREDIENTS

800 g–1 kg (1 lb 12 oz–2 lb 3 oz) watermelon, chopped however you like: big chunks, small chunks, anything goes

1 large Lebanese (short) cucumber, quartered and chopped into wedges

80 g (2¾ oz/½ cup) pitted kalamata or black olives, torn or left whole

150 g (5½ oz/1 cup) Feta (page 197)

large handful of mint leaves (tear any large leaves into smaller pieces)

large handful of dill, roughly torn

½ teaspoon dried oregano

½ red onion, thinly sliced

S&P

Dressing

5 tablespoons extra-virgin olive oil

2 tablespoons red-wine vinegar

1 teaspoon caster (superfine) sugar

Sprinkle a generous pinch of salt over the watermelon, then combine with the remaining ingredients in a large serving bowl. We recommend being heavy-handed with the freshly ground pepper.

Mix all the dressing ingredients together a small bowl, then pour over the salad. Toss to coat well.

THIS SIMPLE, REFRESHING SUMMER SALAD PROVES THAT EVEN THE MOST BASIC RECIPES CAN BE MADE VEGAN WITH LITTLE, EASY TWEAKS.

USE WHATEVER FRESH ASIAN HERBS YOU HAVE. THAI BASIL AND SOME KIND OF MINT ARE IMPERATIVE. THE HERBS ARE A COMPONENT OF THE DISH, NOT A GARNISH.

Larb

Serves 4–6 as a side salad or 2 as a meal (or 1 large meal if you're me)

So whatever you see pictured was most definitely, 100% immediately in my stomach as soon as we approved the shot. The shutter went, we gave a thumbs up and I inhaled this. It's my new favourite. I love describing things as my new favourite to Shannon because it pretty much means every time she's in the kitchen, she's hearing it. But really, everyone, this is my new favourite. At the core, I love Thai food. I would even say it's my favourite cuisine. And it's not even that I crave the Thai dishes I can't have because they're not vegan; I'm happy with my curries, soups and noodles. But when Shannon asked if I'd ever had larb salad, and on hearing I hadn't because there's no way to make it vegan (its main component is ALWAYS meat), it was challenge accepted! (That's the code, right there. Don't tell her there's something she 'can't make vegan'; it sets her right off.) And she mastered it! It's SO FREAKING GOOD.

INGREDIENTS

2 tablespoons Thai sticky rice

3 tablespoons vegetable oil

1 teaspoon grated ginger

1 large garlic clove, minced

1 lemongrass stalk, white part only, very finely sliced

200 g (7 oz/2 cups) soaked TVP (Textured Vegetable Protein) or veggie mince

1 tablespoon pickled chilli or 1 red bird's eye chilli, chopped (we like things spicy, so this recipe is quite spicy as it stands, but feel free to omit or even add more)

juice of 2 limes

2 tablespoons fish sauce

1 teaspoon brown or palm sugar (jaggery)

1 teaspoon sesame oil

½ tablespoon soy sauce

60 ml (2 fl oz/¼ cup) water

1 shallot, halved and thinly sliced

2 kaffir lime leaves, finely shredded

BIG handful of Thai basil

BIG handful of Vietnamese mint

BIG handful of coriander (cilantro)

handful of bean sprouts

200 g (7 oz/1 cup) cherry tomatoes, halved

1 tablespoon roasted peanuts

1 head butter (coral) lettuce (or any pretty little lettuce you can get), washed, plus extra leaves to serve

lime wedges, to serve

Add the sticky rice to a small, dry frying pan (that means no oil!) and toast over a medium heat, stirring constantly, until dark golden brown. Once you've achieved the right colour, transfer to a small bowl and leave to cool. Grind the rice to a fine powder in a mortar and pestle or a blender. Set aside.

Heat the vegetable oil in a large frying pan over a medium–high heat, then add the ginger, garlic and lemongrass. Fry for a minute or so until it begins to turn a light golden colour – NOT DARK. Add the TVP and fry until golden brown and crispy. Once crispy, add a heaped tablespoon of the powdered rice to the mixture and stir to coat.

Stir in the chilli, lime juice, fish sauce, brown sugar, sesame oil, soy sauce and water. Add the shallot and kaffir lime leaf and stir through, keeping the heat nice and high so they are partly cooked. You want them to be semi raw and coated in flavour. Remove from the heat.

In a large bowl, combine your herbs, bean sprouts, cherry tomatoes and peanuts, then add the TVP mixture. Check the flavour and, if needed, add the juice of another half a lime. Add an extra teaspoon of rice powder and mix well to ensure everything is coated.

Arrange the lettuce leaves on a serving dish and pile the larb salad on top. Serve with lime wedges and extra lettuce leaves to eat with.

Panzanella

Serves 4–6 as a side salad

Let's just have a show of hands: who doesn't like bread fried in olive oil? Didn't think so. If you don't have a pulse, maybe. This very clever dish lets you serve fried bread and still call it a salad – brings new definition to being on a salad-only diet, hey? I would dibs this. Health aside, this is such a beautiful, simple-is-best salad. It uses minimal ingredients, keeping the focus on the fresh tomatoes. Only make this salad in the summer when tomatoes are at their best. Made right, this is the most perfect picnic salad. This is also a great way to use up any stale bread in the house.

There are lots of versions of panzanella out there. Some people like cucumber, some like capsicum. You can also ditch the bread and use the rest as a sauce over pasta. Feel free to play, but this is our favourite version.

INGREDIENTS

olive oil, for coating and drizzling

1 large garlic clove

approx. 150 g (5½ oz) day-old bread (but if you have more or less, it doesn't matter)

800 g–1 kg (1 lb 12 oz–2 lb 3 oz) tomatoes (any variety)

½ red onion or 1 large shallot, thinly sliced

1 teaspoon salt

½ fennel bulb, cored and thinly sliced (optional)

large handful of flat-leaf (Italian) parsley leaves

large handful of basil leaves (tear any big leaves)

Dressing

3 tablespoons extra-virgin olive oil

1 tablespoon chopped capers

1 tablespoon balsamic vinegar

S&P

SEASONALITY IS KEY – NEVER EVER MAKE THIS WITH CRAPPY TOMATOES.

Prepare your bread first. Cut your bread into any shape you want. Tear it into rough chunks or cubes, or cut it into rounds. Some like perfectly cut bread, some like it rustic. It's up to you. Coat the base of a large frying pan with a generous amount of olive oil. Smash the garlic clove with the side of your knife and add it to the oil. Set the pan over a medium heat and allow the garlic to sizzle a little.

Add the bread to the pan with the oil. (If all your bread fits in the pan at once, great. If not, work in batches.) Lightly drizzle olive oil on the bread to coat. (We aren't deep-frying the bread here, just toasting it.) Toast, flipping over regularly, until golden and crispy on all sides. Remove and leave to cool while you prep the tomatoes.

Our preference is to cut the tomatoes into different shapes, some in wedges, some rounds, etc. If they're small, just cut them in half or keep them whole. Combine the tomatoes and onion in a bowl with the salt. Mix well and set aside to allow the salt to draw some of the moisture out of the tomatoes. This will help the dressing adhere.

For the dressing, whisk all the ingredients together in a small bowl.

Transfer the bread to a salad bowl and mix with the tomatoes, fennel and herbs. Pour over the dressing and toss to coat, then check the seasoning before serving.

Sushi Salad

Serves 4–6 as a side salad

This salad is actually the inside of an avocado roll. It's like eating a giant bowl-sized avocado sushi roll, but better. It's hands down one of the best and best-selling salads at the Deli. Scratch that: it's the best Deli item there is. As in, people line up for this in the same way they line up for their favourite doughnuts, and they're always disappointed when we sell out.

If you want to make this more of a meal, don't be afraid to throw in some vegan prawns or tuna, etc. For some crunchy added fun, toss in some wasabi peas.

INGREDIENTS

200 g (7 oz/1 cup) long-grain rice, cooked and cooled

95 g (3¼ oz/½ cup) black rice, cooked and cooled

1 avocado, stone removed, cut into 1 cm (½ in) cubes

50 g (1¾ oz/⅓ cup) Japanese pink pickled ginger

1 Lebanese (short) cucumber, quartered, seeds removed and flesh diced

2 handfuls of snow pea (mangetout) sprouts, torn (or whatever greens you like)

10 g (¼ oz) dried seaweed, soaked in water to rehydrate then roughly chopped (whatever your favourite variety is; see Note)

1 tablespoon white sesame seeds

1 tablespoon black sesame seeds

Dressing

1 nori (seaweed) sheet

½ tablespoon sesame oil

160 g (5½ oz/⅔ cup) Mayonnaise (page 200)

1½ tablespoons rice-wine vinegar

2 tablespoons juice from the pickled ginger

2 teaspoons soy sauce

1 teaspoon salt

First, make the dressing. On a gas stove, turn a flame on high and pass the nori sheet over the fire until it starts to curl and toast. If you don't have a gas stove, put the sheet in a dry frying pan and turn it until crispy. Blitz to a powder in a blender, or grind it in a mortar and pestle.

In a bowl, mix the nori powder with all the remaining dressing ingredients until well combined.

Combine all the salad ingredients in a bowl, pour over the dressing and toss to coat. Serve cold.

Note: When we say your favourite seaweed, we mean it: use kelp, wakame, anything. Or you can use a pre-made seaweed salad. If you do, use a minimum of 100 g (3½ oz) but, really, as much as you want.

NORI POWDER IS AN AWESOME CULINARY SECRET WEAPON, ESPECIALLY FOR ANY DISH REQUIRING A LITTLE EXTRA SALTINESS.

THIS SALAD CAN BE EATEN HOT OR
COLD. IF YOU WANT IT HOT, JUST
KEEP YOUR NOODLES HOT.

Thai Peanut Noodle Salad

Serves 4–6 as a side salad

The creation of this salad really tests the satay sauce theory: that you only stay away from this marvellous creation if you're allergic to peanuts. Everyone loves satay sauce and a Thai peanut noodle salad is up everyone's alley, especially when it's either really hot outside or you need something to remind you of being on holiday. Please use whatever veggies are your favourite; this is the time to craft a salad that suits your personal taste. Make it a salad you want to eat the entire bowl of and not share with anyone.

INGREDIENTS

any combination of vegetables you like, shredded (our favourites are carrot, capsicum, spring onions/scallions, snow peas/mangetout, Chinese cabbage/wombok, bok choy/pak choy, enoki mushrooms, bean sprouts, Thai basil, Vietnamese mint, coriander/cilantro)

200 g (7 oz) vermicelli rice noodles, cooked and cooled (follow the packet instructions; don't cool the noodles if you want a warm salad)

crispy shallots, to garnish

crushed roasted peanuts, to garnish

pickled or fresh chilli, to garnish

any style of tofu, mock prawns or chicken (optional)

Dressing

250 ml (8½ fl oz/1 cup) Satay Sauce (page 205)

juice of 2 limes

To make the dressing, combine the satay sauce and lime juice in a bowl and thin the mixture out with enough water to achieve your desired consistency (approximately ¼ cup water).

Put your selection of prepared veg in a bowl with the noodles, add as much of the dressing as you like, then toss to coat. Garnish with crispy shallots, crushed peanuts and chilli. Add tofu, prawns or chicken, if desired.

HEARTY SOUPS

Soup is our favourite meal. If we could ensure we would both be eating soup for the rest of our lives, we'd be happy. Please don't write soup off as a typical vegan meal. It's not. We've chosen, trimmed and curated our favourite soups here. But even now, there are so many more we could include. (Another book for another day, perhaps.)

Some ground rules about soup. It's always good to have it on the go in the fridge. You can always freeze soup for another day and soup always gets better with time.

The disclaimer on these recipes: they make big batches and they are all pretty damn good for you! ALL GOOD NEWS for your future self. Our final piece of advice: with every soup recipe you must always serve large, large quantities of delicious fresh bread.

Mulligatawny

Serves 4–6

This soup goes way, way back – 1870s way back. It is, as some say, one of the few good things to come out of Britain's colonial past. It's a hybrid dish of fragrant Indian flavours and colonial adaptations that suited more 'refined' English tastes. Colonial rule dictated soup must be eaten at every meal, so Indian cooks created a more decadent version of their madrassi by adding meat and vegetables to the thin, spicy broth, which was typically served with rice. Though the original was probably a hit, the mulligatawny we know today – adapted over centuries – is one we much appreciate. And though it's often overlooked on Indian restaurant menus, this soup is such a winner. Hold on, I want mulligatawny now. BRB.

INGREDIENTS

2 tablespoons vegetable or coconut oil

2 tablespoons butter

1 brown onion, finely diced

2 garlic cloves, minced

1 tablespoon grated ginger

2 green chillies, sliced into rings (seeds removed for a milder soup)

1 teaspoon salt

2 teaspoons ground cumin

2 teaspoons ground coriander

1 teaspoon garam masala

1 teaspoon ground turmeric

½ teaspoon ground cardamom

1 large carrot, finely diced

2 celery stalks, finely diced

1 large green apple, peeled and finely diced

375 g (13 oz/1½ cups) dried red lentils

1.5 litres (51 fl oz/6 cups) vegetable or chicken stock

250 ml (8½ fl oz/1 cup) coconut milk

juice of ½ lemon

185 g (6½ oz/1 cup) cooked jasmine rice

handful of coriander (cilantro), chopped

S&P

Heat the oil and butter in a large saucepan over a medium heat and gently fry the onion until golden and soft. Add the garlic, ginger, chilli and salt and cook for 1 minute. Stir in the cumin, coriander, garam masala, turmeric, cardamom and plenty of salt and pepper, and fry over a low heat until fragrant.

Add the carrot, celery and apple and fry until they begin to soften, then add the lentils and stock and bring to the boil. Reduce the heat to low and simmer until the lentils are mushy.

Mix in the coconut milk, lemon juice, rice and chopped coriander, then simmer for another 10 minutes. Season to taste.

Photo page 060.

Cauliflower & Celeriac

Serves 4–6

Simply put, this soup is luxurious – and full of veg. The silky texture lends itself to many delicious additions when plating: a splash of truffle oil, crispy bacon bits, snipped chives or a good crack of fresh black pepper. It's just the best. Plus, it's always good to play around with celeriac, especially if you've never had a go with it. It has all the good qualities of celery, but it's a starchy root veg. And oh does it go well with cauliflower! You'll be surprised to know this soup has no cream in it. What a revelation.

INGREDIENTS

80 ml (2½ fl oz/⅓ cup) extra-virgin olive oil

1 large brown onion, diced

1 small cauliflower head, roughly chopped

1 large celeriac, peeled and diced

1 teaspoon caraway seeds

3 garlic cloves, minced

80 ml (2½ fl oz/⅓ cup) white wine

1 bay leaf

3 thyme sprigs

1 rosemary sprig

approx. 1 litre (34 fl oz/4 cups) chicken stock, to cover

2 tablespoons butter

salt & white pepper

Heat the oil in a large saucepan over a medium heat and slowly cook the onion until soft and lightly golden.

Add the cauliflower, celeriac, caraway seeds and garlic and cook until softened. Season with salt and pepper.

Add all the remaining ingredients, except the butter, and simmer on low until the vegetables are very soft. Remove the bay leaf, thyme sprig and rosemary sprig, add the butter and blend in a high-speed blender until smooth. Check and adjust the seasoning, then serve.

Photo page 060.

MULLIGATAWNY

Sweet Potato, Chipotle & Orange

Serves 4–6

Soup season is by far the best season, and the effort that goes into making soup from scratch is the best effort of all. Sweet potato soup and a pantry stocked with fresh, crusty bread fully sets you up for the cold weather. The additions of chipotle and orange make this soup smokier and brighter in the best ways possible.

INGREDIENTS

60 ml (2 fl oz/¼ cup) extra-virgin olive oil

1 red onion, roughly diced

1 celery stalk, roughly diced

½ red capsicum (bell pepper), roughly diced

2 large garlic cloves, minced

1½ teaspoons ground cumin

1 bay leaf

1 teaspoon dried oregano

1 chipotle in adobo sauce, roughly chopped

1 kg (2 lb 3 oz) sweet potato, peeled and chopped

750 ml (25½ fl oz/3 cups) vegetable or chicken stock

¼ bunch of coriander (cilantro), roughly chopped, plus extra to serve

zest and juice of ½ orange

125 g (4½ oz/½ cup) sour cream, plus extra to serve

juice of 1 lime

S&P

Heat the oil in a large saucepan over a medium heat and fry the onion, celery and capsicum. Season lightly with salt and pepper and gently cook until soft and slightly golden. Add the garlic and cook for another minute.

Add the cumin, bay leaf, oregano and chipotle and cook for another minute, then add the sweet potato and stir to coat. Pour in enough stock to just cover the sweet potato, then simmer over a low heat until soft.

Once the sweet potato is soft, remove the bay leaf, then add the coriander, orange zest and juice, and blend until smooth with a regular or hand-held blender. Pour the soup into a clean pot and add the sour cream. Stir until well combined.

Add the lime juice and check the seasoning, adding more salt and pepper to taste.

Top with a little extra coriander and more sour cream, if you like.

Photo page 061.

Minestrone

Serves 4–6

Yet another classic soup made better by Shannon. Minestrone as you know it can often be watery, flavourless, over or under salted and just plain sad – full of flaccid veg. It should be called flaccid soup. Yuck. This is the opposite of that.

This minestrone is for that soup hater in your life who claims that soup isn't a meal. This is that middle finger of a soup: thick, heavy-duty and guaranteed to stick some meat on your bones (don't mind the expression). Anytime you throw pasta into a soup, you'll have our vote. Pasta can really do no wrong, and when you combine it with another thing that you love (soup), the end result will be very, very good. In a pinch, you can use any kind of pasta you want, even if you only have spaghetti or lasagne sheets – just break them up into bits.

Also – important sidenote – don't skimp on the parmesan garnish.

INGREDIENTS

80 ml (2½ fl oz/⅓ cup) extra-virgin olive oil

1 brown onion, diced

2 celery stalks, sliced

1 large carrot, cut into 1 cm (½ in) dice

½ bulb fennel, cored and cut into 1 cm (½ in) dice

1 teaspoon chilli flakes (optional)

3 garlic cloves, minced

1 teaspoon fresh or dried oregano

400 g (14 oz) fresh or tinned diced tomatoes

½ red capsicum (bell pepper), cut into 1 cm (½ in) dice (approx. ½ cup)

10 g (¼ oz/½ cup) dried porcini mushrooms, soaked in boiling water for 10 minutes, then drained and roughly chopped

125 g (4½ oz/½ cup) dried red lentils

2 litres (68 fl oz/8 cups) vegetable or chicken stock

8 stalks cavolo nero (Tuscan kale), roughly chopped (approx. 2 cups)

1 small zucchini (courgette), diced

60 g (2 oz/½ cup) green beans, sliced

1 bay leaf

1 x 400 g (14 oz) tin chickpeas, borlotti or white beans

1 tablespoon nutritional yeast

155 g (5½ oz/1 cup) uncooked tubetti or other small tube pasta

S&P

30 g (1 oz/1 cup) basil leaves, torn, to garnish

30 g (1 oz/½ cup) flat-leaf (Italian) parsley, chopped, to garnish

parmesan, to garnish

When chopping your veg, keep it all pretty much the same size.

Heat the oil in large saucepan over a medium heat. Add the onion, celery, carrot, fennel and a big pinch of salt. Fry until the veg begins to soften and appears lightly golden in colour.

Add the chilli flakes, garlic, oregano and tomato and cook for 2 minutes. Add all the remaining ingredients except the pasta and fresh herbs. Continue cooking over a low heat, uncovered, for about 30 minutes, stirring occasionally. Add the pasta and simmer until cooked.

Finish by adding the fresh herbs, then check the seasoning. Garnish liberally with parmesan.

Photo page 065.

MUSHROOM & BARLEY

SPLIT
PEA

MINESTRONE

Split Pea

Serves 4–6

This seemingly easy vegetable soup is constantly ruined by a giant ham hock. Unnecessary, says Shannon, as she has crafted up this amazing, full-bodied, smoky soup exactly replicating the texture and smokiness that ham would provide. She has literally created that mouthfeel illusion, but without any mock-meat substitute, and certainly no ham. She has simply nailed the flavours using pure veg and a little help from that magical ingredient, liquid smoke.

INGREDIENTS

80 ml (2½ fl oz/⅓ cup) extra-virgin olive oil

1 brown onion, diced

1 large carrot, diced

2 celery stalks, diced

½ fennel bulb, diced

2 tablespoons minced garlic

1 tablespoon porcini powder

190 g (6½ oz/1½ cups) green split peas

125 ml (4 fl oz/½ cup) white wine

1.5 litres (51 fl oz/6 cups) vegetable or chicken stock

1 bay leaf

3 thyme sprigs

1 rosemary sprig

1 teaspoon liquid smoke

S&P

handful of dill, chopped, to garnish

Heat the oil in a large saucepan over a medium heat and fry the onion, carrot, celery, fennel, garlic and porcini powder until soft and lightly golden.

Add the remaining ingredients and bring to the boil, then reduce the heat and simmer for approximately 30–45 minutes, or until the peas are soft and mushy. If the soup appears too dry at this point, add up to another 250 ml (8½ fl oz/1 cup) stock. (Some split peas are drier than others and absorb more liquid.) Remove the bay leaf, thyme sprig and rosemary sprig, season with salt and pepper and garnish with the dill.

Photo page 065.

PORCINI POWDER IS A SECRET WEAPON OF THE VEGAN WORLD; IT MAKES THINGS TASTE EXTRA MEATY.

Mushroom & Barley

Serves 4–6

I'm a real meal-on-the-go kind of a gal, without the time to cook or prep meals, but also a mega soup fanatic, so the grab-n-go vegan mushroom and barley soup from Wholefoods in the States was my favourite. I loved how meaty the mushrooms tasted but, best, I was eating something that was healthy and filling: two things that rarely go together in my busy life. Simply start a sentence with, 'What I really miss is …' and Shannon stops what she is doing and goes to get the ingredients to cook it. She not only nailed this soup, but made it even better. This mushroom and barley soup is full of flavour, and its velvety richness coats the mouth and hits the spot.

INGREDIENTS

3 tablespoons butter

1 brown onion, diced

1 carrot, diced

2 celery stalks, diced

270 g (9½ oz/3 cups) button mushrooms, sliced

10 g (¼ oz) dried shiitake mushrooms soaked in boiling water (reserve 250 ml/8½ fl oz/1 cup soaking liquid)

10 g (¼ oz) dried porcini mushrooms soaked in boiling water (reserve 250 ml/8½ fl oz/1 cup soaking liquid)

2 garlic cloves, minced

2 teaspoons chopped thyme leaves

1 bay leaf

½ teaspoon chilli flakes (optional)

220 g (8 oz/1 cup) pearled barley

80 ml (2½ fl oz/⅓ cup) white wine

1 litre (34 fl oz/4 cups) vegetable or beef stock

handful of flat-leaf (Italian) parsley, chopped, to garnish

S&P

Heat the butter in a large saucepan over a medium heat and add the vegetables and garlic. Cook until soft and golden.

Add the thyme, bay leaf, chilli flakes (if using) and barley, and stir well to coat. Deglaze the pan with the wine, then add the stock and reserved mushroom soaking liquid. Bring to the boil, then simmer until the barley is soft. Remove the bay leaf.

Add the parsley and season with salt and pepper to taste.

Photo page 064.

Corn Congee

Serves 4–6

The dawn of congee in the West is near, according to Shannon. If you ever find Shannon eating anything that resembles breakfast, it will be this traditional Asian rice porridge, known as congee. It's one of her favourite things ever, ever, ever. It's also one of the most misunderstood ready-meals at the Deli. Shannon's new personal mission is to destroy the ramen craze with congee. The great thing about congee is that once you've made it, you can add anything you want to it. Literally, garnish it however you like.

If you've never had congee before, it's more like a porridge than a risotto; you're meant to overcook it. Make it for breakfast, a late-night snack or as a hangover cure.

INGREDIENTS

2 tablespoons vegetable oil

1 teaspoon sesame oil, plus extra to garnish

4 large spring onions (scallions), white and green parts, finely sliced, plus extra to garnish

2 garlic cloves, minced

20 g (¾ oz) ginger, peeled and julienned

1 star anise

1 x 420 g (15 oz) tin creamed corn

150 g (5½ oz/¾ cup) jasmine rice

3 tablespoons Shaoxing wine or dry sherry

1 tablespoon light soy sauce

1 litre (34 fl oz/4 cups) vegetable or chicken stock

freshly sliced chilli or chilli oil, to garnish (optional)

Pickled Chinese Mushrooms, to garnish (optional, but highly recommended) (page 037)

Heat both oils in a saucepan over a medium heat. Sweat off the spring onion, garlic and ginger until soft, then add the star anise. Cook for another minute, then add the corn, stir again and cook for another 2 minutes.

Add the rice and stir to coat. Add the wine and soy sauce and cook out for 30 seconds. Pour the stock over the rice and bring to a simmer. Reduce the heat to low and cook, stirring regularly to avoid the rice sticking, for 45 minutes to 1 hour, or until the rice is very soft and beginning to fall apart. Add a little extra stock if needed during cooking. Remove the star anise.

Garnish with extra sliced spring onion and a drizzle of sesame oil. If you like it hot, add some fresh chilli or chilli oil. Definitely go to the effort of making the pickled mushrooms – they're worth it.

Thai Curry Pumpkin & Coconut

Serves 4–6

Forget what you know about pumpkin soups and Thai curries. This soup is a knockout. When you're talking about soup perfection, this is it. Thai flavours are ones that have never, in our opinion, been properly introduced to pumpkin soups in the past. The richness, smoothness and decadence of this soup makes you look ultra fancy in the kitchen, but wait until your guests see you licking the pot after you've served up. There ain't nothing fancy about that. It seems like a lot of ingredients and a few more steps than your usual pumpkin soup, but it's worth every minute.

INGREDIENTS

2 tablespoons coconut oil

2 brown onions, diced

1 green chilli, sliced

1 tablespoon grated ginger

2 garlic cloves, minced

1½ heaped tablespoons curry paste (your favourite paste: red, yellow, whatever)

1 small butternut pumpkin (squash) or ½ Japanese pumpkin (approx. 1 kg/2 lb 3 oz), peeled and roughly chopped

1 litre (34 fl oz/4 cups) chicken stock

2 pandan leaves, cut in half and knotted (optional)

1 tablespoon fish sauce

handful of coriander (cilantro) stalks

4 whole kaffir lime leaves

250 ml (8½ fl oz/1 cup) coconut milk

S&P

small handful of coriander (cilantro) leaves, to garnish

juice of 1 lime, to serve

Heat the oil in a large saucepan and fry the onion, chilli, ginger and garlic until soft. Add the curry paste and cook out for 1 minute, then add the pumpkin and stir until well coated.

Pour the stock over the pumpkin and add the pandan leaves, fish sauce, coriander stalks and kaffir lime leaves. Simmer over a medium heat until the pumpkin is very soft, then add the coconut milk and continue simmering for a further 5 minutes.

Remove the pandan and kaffir lime leaves, then blend until smooth using a regular or hand-held blender. Season to taste, then finish with coriander leaves and lime juice.

Pho

Serves 4–8, depending on how much broth y'all like

What a great day it is that pho no longer needs an intro; it's as ubiquitous as split pea or lentil soup. People even know how to eat it with the proper garnishes – herbs, bean sprouts and all. But there's always one thing missing: fish sauce, even if you can get a vegan version. And if there's one thing we can learn from Shannon, it's not the (non-vegan) things you take out, but the (vegan) things you don't put back in. It's those crucial elements, my friends, that make pho, pho. So, make it properly or pho-ck you. (Can't resist a good pho pun.)

INGREDIENTS

Pho Stock

10 cm (4 in) piece of ginger

1 large brown onion

1 head of garlic

¼ pineapple

2 lemongrass stems, smashed with the side of a knife

2 green chillies, split in half lengthways

1 large carrot, sliced

2 celery stalks

1 large leek, split in half lengthways

6 whole cloves

1 cinnamon stick

2 star anise

2 tablespoons white peppercorns

½ bunch of dill stalks (optional)

½ bunch of coriander (cilantro) stalks

½ bunch of spring onions (scallions), roughly chopped

1 orange, halved

125 ml (4 fl oz/½ cup) fish sauce

10 cm (4 in) piece of kombu (optional)

4 whole dried shiitake mushrooms

2 tablespoons beef stock powder

5 litres (169 fl oz/21 cups) water

Pho (continued)

Suggested veg and meat

red onion, sliced

carrot

broccoli florets

bok choy (pak choy)

vegan chicken or any style of tofu you love in pho

To serve

rice noodles

Sriracha

hoisin sauce

Suggested garnishes

bean sprouts

Thai basil

Vietnamese mint or common mint

coriander (cilantro)

lemon wedges

chilli, freshly sliced

Char your vegetables. If you can get your hands on one, a griddle pan works best. Set the pan over the highest heat to make it mega, mega hot. Turn your extraction fan on high, disable the fire alarm, open all the windows.

Cut the ginger in half lengthways and place it, cut side down, on the hot griddle. Halve the onion, keeping the skin on, and add it to the griddle. Cut the entire head of garlic in half horizontally, exposing the cloves, and place it, cut side down, on the griddle. Cut the pineapple into thirds and place each chunk, cut side down, on the griddle. Burn the shit out of everything. Make everything go black. Not light golden brown – black. Turn everything over and char the other side roughly. The onions may be tough, but char as much as you can; it doesn't matter if the other side isn't completely black.

Combine the rest of the base ingredients in your biggest heavy-based pot (big enough to hold 5 litres/170 fl oz/20 cups) and bring to the boil. Reduce the heat to a low simmer and keep an eye on it for 2–3 hours. It might sound like a lot of liquid, but the stock will reduce and concentrate down to approximately 4 litres (135 fl oz/16 cups). And seriously, don't skimp on the cooking time; 1 hour will be good, but the flavour won't be fully developed.

Once the stock is cooked, carefully strain it through a colander into a clean bowl and discard the solids. That's the base for your pho.

At this point, you can serve it straight away. Definitely keep some for your dinner and set the rest aside to cool. Once cool, store in airtight freezer bags and freeze for other days of rad pho eating.

To build the soup, start by cooking the rice noodles according to the packet instructions – about 25 g (1 oz) per serve. Once the noodles have soaked and finished cooking, divide them between the serving bowls.

Measure out about 500 ml (17 fl oz/2 cups) of broth per person into a saucepan and bring to the boil. Add whatever veg you like, plus anything else you want: vegan chicken strips, firm fried tofu – or any tofu really (tofu puffs, silken, firm) – cut into bite-sized pieces.

Serve the soup alongside big plates of garnishes, Sriracha and hoisin sauce. Encourage everyone to go ham on the fresh herbs, bean sprouts, chilli and lemon.

Lentil

Serves 4–6

Yeah, yeah. Lentil soup. Vegan book. That's all us vegans eat anyway, right? Lentils and grass. You've had lentil soup before? Everyone's mum or gran made a version of this, anywhere and everywhere in the world. It's amazing that no matter where you are, you'll find a version of lentil soup. But you haven't really, because you haven't had this one. Why is it so good? I can't even put my finger on it. It just is. Considering the excitement that echoes through the Deli over this soup, you would think there was a new flavour of doughnut coming through; but no, lentil soup. The best damn lentil soup you've ever had.

INGREDIENTS

80 ml (2½ fl oz/⅓ cup) extra-virgin olive oil, plus extra to garnish

2 celery stalks, diced

1 carrot, diced

1 brown onion, diced

½ fennel bulb, diced

2 tablespoons capers, chopped

2 tablespoons minced garlic

2 teaspoons chilli flakes

1 teaspoon smoked paprika

250 ml (8½ fl oz/1 cup) red wine

185 g (6½ oz/1 cup) dried green lentils

375 g (13 oz/1½ cups) dried red lentils

2 litres (68 fl oz/8 cups) vegetable or chicken stock

handful of flat-leaf (Italian) parsley, chopped

handful of basil, chopped

S&P

Heat the oil in a large saucepan over a medium heat and add all the vegetables except the garlic. Fry until soft and slightly golden, then add the capers, garlic, chilli and paprika and cook for 1 minute.

Deglaze the pan with the wine, then add the green and red lentils, stir to coat, and pour in the stock. Bring to the boil, then reduce the heat and simmer until the lentils have broken down and become very soft. Once the lentils are cooked, add the herbs and season with salt and pepper. Add a glug of olive oil and stir through.

Photo page 078.

LENTIL SCHMENTIL!
DON'T KNOCK IT 'TIL
YOU'VE TRIED IT.

Spicy Piquillo Pepper & Chickpea

Serves 4–6

What a crazy notion it is to declare you would eat something forever. But the entire time this soup was on the menu at the restaurant – a (long-running) winter menu of 2017 – I ate it every single shift and loved it so much we brought it over to the Deli to sell as a take-home meal. I'd like to say this was one of our bestsellers at the restaurant, but that would be a lie. People don't love soup the same way Shannon and I love soup, and that's just a fact. But, for all the people who did eat it, they understood it. So, to those people, congratulations! You got what you wanted and you and I both will be making this soup literally all the time.

P.S. Don't be scared by the word 'spicy'; it's not that hot. But if you do like it hot, add some brutally hot sauce to raise the heat.

INGREDIENTS

60 ml (2 fl oz/¼ cup) extra-virgin olive oil

1 brown onion, blitzed (but not mushy)

1 heaped tablespoon minced garlic

1 long red chilli, sliced

500 g (1 lb 2 oz) piquillo peppers

1 x 400 g (14 oz) tin chickpeas (reserve the chickpea liquid for making Cherry Meringue Pie, page 165)

½ teaspoon cumin seeds

1 litre (34 fl oz/4 cups) chicken stock

1½ tablespoons hot sauce

zest and juice of 1 large lemon

300 g (10½ oz/1½ cups) cooked medium- or long-grain rice

S&P

roasted chickpeas (see Note), to garnish

piquillo pepper strips, chopped, to garnish

flat-leaf (Italian) parsley, to garnish

extra-virgin olive oil, to garnish

Heat the oil in a large saucepan over a low heat and fry the onion, garlic and chilli until soft. Add the peppers, chickpeas, cumin seeds and some salt and pepper, and cook for a further 10 minutes.

Blend the ingredients using a regular or hand-held blender until very smooth, then slowly add the stock, hot sauce and lemon zest and juice. Check the seasoning, adding more hot sauce and lemon juice if needed. Add the rice and mix well.

Garnish your bowls with roasted chickpeas, piquillo pepper strips, chopped parsley and olive oil.

Notes: To make roasted chickpeas, heat some olive oil in a frying pan over a medium heat and fry your garnish chickpeas until crispy. Add a big pinch of salt, ground cumin and paprika, and stir well to evenly coat.

If you can't get piquillo peppers, you can substitute roasted sweet red peppers. Capsicums (bell peppers), or bullhorns with seeds – jarred or tinned – are fine too.

Photo page 079.

Smoky Potato & Leek

Serves 4–6

We can say, without a shred of arrogance, this soup is a no-brainer. Try to find someone who doesn't like mashed potatoes or hot chips. Potatoes always win. Always. So, when they're blended with some beautiful velvety vegetables and herbs, it's like a big, fluffy blanket for your insides. This soup makes us want the weather to turn cold, just so we can have an excuse to make it and eat an entire pot. (Wait a sec, we can make this soup, turn on the AC and pretend it's really cold outside.) In fact, we don't need excuses; this soup is good anytime, all the time.

INGREDIENTS

1 tablespoon extra-virgin olive oil

2 tablespoons butter

2 large leeks, white and lightest green parts only,
  halved lengthways and sliced

2 garlic cloves, minced

1 teaspoon chopped thyme leaves

1 teaspoon chopped rosemary leaves

125 ml (4 fl oz/½ cup) white wine

4 large potatoes, peeled and diced
  (approx. 1 kg/2 lb 3 oz)

1 litre (34 fl oz/4 cups) chicken stock

125 ml (4 fl oz/½ cup) unsweetened soy milk

⅓ block smoked tofu, sliced into small strips, or
  Rice Paper Bacon (optional) (page 194)

salt & white pepper

Heat the oil and butter in a large saucepan over a medium heat and slowly cook the leeks until very soft. Add the garlic and herbs and cook for another minute.

Deglaze the pan with the wine, then add the potatoes and stock. Simmer over a low heat until the potatoes are very soft. Add the soy milk and blend the soup using a regular or hand-held blender. Check the seasoning.

If using, fry the tofu or bacon in oil until crispy, then fold it through the finished soup.

Photo page 078.

LENTIL

POTATO &
LEEK

SPICY PIQUILLO PEPPER
& CHICKPEA

Borscht

Serves 4–6

Beetroots are simply incomparable, especially when it comes to this traditional Eastern European favourite; it's one of those amazing veg-based soups that doesn't compare to any other. Shannon's love affair with borscht, beige food and dill began at New York's Ukrainian institution, Veselka. It was the early 2000s, a time when not much Eastern Euro food existed in Australia, and it cast a whole new light on Shannon's obsession with potatoes and onions. Who needs colour, anyway? Except when it comes to this soup – then red is permissible.

INGREDIENTS

60 ml (2 fl oz/¼ cup) extra-virgin olive oil

1 brown onion, sliced

1 carrot, diced

2 celery stalks, diced

1 parsnip, peeled and diced

3 garlic cloves, minced

2 teaspoons caraway seeds

1 teaspoon allspice

½ teaspoon ground cloves

1 teaspoon thyme leaves

250 g (9 oz/1 cup) diced tomatoes

185 ml (6 fl oz/¾ cup) beer (anything light)

150 g (5½ oz/2 cups) red cabbage, finely shredded

2 tablespoons porcini powder

10 g (¼ oz/¼ cup) dried mixed mushrooms, blitzed to a powder using a high-speed or regular blender

3 tablespoons apple-cider vinegar

1 tablespoon brown sugar

1 bay leaf

2 litres (68 fl oz/8 cups) vegetable or beef stock

1 kg (2 lb 3 oz) beetroot, peeled and grated

½ bunch of dill, chopped, plus extra to serve

S&P

sour cream, to serve

Heat the oil in a large saucepan over a medium heat and fry the onion, carrot, celery, parsnip and garlic until softened and starting to colour. Season with salt and pepper.

Add the spices, thyme and tomatoes and cook until softened and starting to colour. Pour in the beer and allow to reduce slightly.

Add the cabbage, porcini powder, dried mushrooms, vinegar, brown sugar, bay leaf and stock. Simmer on a low heat for about 30 minutes. Check the seasoning, then add the beetroot and cook for another hour. Once the soup has finished cooking, stir through the dill and remove the bay leaf.

Serve with extra dill, black pepper and sour cream.

CHOC HAZELNUT
EXCESS FRAPPÉ

Think BLITZED FERRERO
ROCHER!!

S. CINNAMON
— CHOC
— WHITE

DELICIOUS
Ready -meals

Now's the time to reclaim your favourites. It's time to recreate those special dishes your gran and mum made you. Gone is the hopelessness of never being able to enjoy your family's hearty classics, or relive those beautiful childhood memories with food.

The amount of cookbooks Shannon buys is, as she puts it, 'borderline ridiculous, shameful, really'. However, in cookbooks both vegan and non, people aren't veganising some very basic, fundamental and amazing dishes. Speculating that replacing flavours or textures may be too daunting for some, this is Shannon's call to action. Gone are the Christmases when you don't have any options beyond the crappy, wilted side veg dishes or token 'salads' where you still have to pick out the cheese. Shannon's done the work for you and now it's your time to shine.

Beef Bourguignon

Serves 4–6

Move over Julia Child; we have vegan beef bourguignon coming your way. Most wouldn't dream of replacing the main component of this classic French stew with a veggie substitute, but we did and this was the result. Same beautiful, rich mouthfeel, but without cholesterol. Serve this up with traditional accompaniments – creamy mash and green beans – or do as we do at the Deli and fill your pies with it (aka the best pie filling of all time; see How to Make Pies on page 132). A warning: no matter how much you make, it's virtually impossible to 'save some for later'.

Let's talk beef. Beef = not beef. Whatever brand of vegan meat replacement you prefer/can get, use it. Anything resembling a chunk of beef. If vegan beef isn't available, bulk it out with the same quantity of mushrooms. It won't be the same, but it will still be super yum.

INGREDIENTS

80 ml (2½ fl oz/1/3 cup) extra-virgin olive oil

1 large brown onion, diced

1 carrot, diced

220 g (8 oz/2 cups) button mushrooms, whole or halved

2 celery stalks, diced

2 garlic cloves, minced

10 g (¼ oz/1 cup) mixed dried mushrooms, soaked (reserve 250 ml/8½ fl oz/1 cup soaking liquid)

1 tablespoon chopped rosemary leaves

1 tablespoon chopped thyme leaves

handful of flat-leaf (Italian) parsley, roughly chopped

1½ tablespoons tomato paste (concentrated purée)

1 tablespoon butter

2 tablespoons plain (all-purpose) flour

375 ml (12½ fl oz/1½ cups) red wine

250 g (9 oz) beef pieces

1 tablespoon soy sauce

1 teaspoon dijon mustard

S&P

Heat the oil in a large saucepan over a medium heat and fry the onion, carrot, mushroom and celery until soft and slightly golden.

Add the garlic and cook out for 1 minute, then add the rehydrated mushrooms, herbs, tomato paste, butter and flour. Cook out the flour for 1 minute, then deglaze the pan with the wine.

Mix in the remaining ingredients and bring to the boil, then reduce the heat to low and simmer for 45 minutes. Season with salt and pepper.

Chilli

Serves 4–6

Good lord, do we love chilli. It's the borderline meal-soup-stew dish with all the necessary elements: heat, beans and Mexican flavours. And it's bloody filling. This version is our favourite. Could it be the chocolate? Could it be the coffee? Who knows.

This chilli is also a great pie filling (see How to Make Pies on page 132; just add the cheese before topping with pastry). Use it as a topping for nachos, as a filling for burritos or quesadillas, over rice, over quinoa, or with corn chips and queso. Or just straight up with ALL THE TOPPINGS.

INGREDIENTS

80 ml (2½ fl oz/⅓ cup) extra-virgin olive oil

1 large brown onion, diced

1 red capsicum (bell pepper), diced

1 celery stalk, diced

½ jalapeño chilli, diced (seeds removed for a milder chilli)

1 poblano pepper, diced (optional)

3 garlic cloves, minced

2 teaspoons ground coriander

1½ teaspoons cumin seeds

2 teaspoons smoked paprika

pinch of ground cloves (optional)

2 chipotles in adobo sauce

200 g (7 oz/2 cups) soaked TVP (Textured Vegetable Protein) or veggie mince

400 g (14 oz) fresh or tinned diced tomatoes

500 ml (17 fl oz/2 cups) vegetable or beef stock

1 cinnamon stick

1 tablespoon soy sauce

80 ml (2½ fl oz/⅓ cup) freshly brewed black coffee (hot or cold will do; even cold-brew or instant coffee will work)

240 g (8½ oz/2 cups) tinned or cooked dried kidney or black beans

2 tablespoons dark chocolate chips

200 g (7 oz/1 cup) fresh or frozen corn kernels

handful of coriander (cilantro), stalks and leaves separated, chopped

S&P

hot sauce, to serve (optional)

1 teaspoon chilli powder (optional)

Our favourite toppings for chilli

Use all, use a few, use none; this chilli is your chilli to do what you want with!

diced red onion

cheese

sour cream

diced avo, or guac

chives

coriander (cilantro)

Heat the oil in a large saucepan over a medium heat and fry the onion, capsicum, celery, jalapeño, poblano and garlic until soft, then add the spices and chipotle.

Add the TVP and stir to coat, then stir in the tomatoes, stock, cinnamon stick, soy sauce and coffee. Bring to the boil, then reduce the heat to low and simmer for about 30 minutes, stirring occasionally so it doesn't stick. If it begins to dry out, add a splash more stock. If you prefer a thicker chilli, don't add extra stock. The texture will also depend on how much liquid the TVP absorbs, so keep an eye on it.

After 20 minutes, add your beans, choc chips, corn and chopped coriander stalks, and continue cooking for the remaining 10 minutes. Check the seasoning and finish with chopped coriander leaves and, if using, hot sauce and chilli powder.

Note: This recipe already packs a bit of heat, but if you want it super spicy, add the hot sauce, chilli powder and more chipotles. If you prefer it milder, halve the spicy ingredients.

Broccoli, Lemon & Mint Risotto

Serves 4–6

Death to the bland, boring, overcooked, undercooked, crappy, token veg option on the menu: risotto. Seriously, how can this dish be so consistently underwhelming? We are uncertain, but what we do know is how to do it right. Sure, you have your mushroom risottos, but here we have taken it up a notch, and we can help you step up your risotto game, too. This one is undeniably good and a really pretty colour. Step it up, friends.

INGREDIENTS

60 ml (2 fl oz/¼ cup) extra-virgin olive oil

½ brown onion, finely diced

3 spring onions (scallions), white and green parts, chopped

1–1.25 litres (34–42 fl oz/4–5 cups) vegetable stock

1 garlic clove, minced

330 g (11½ oz/1½ cups) arborio rice

80 g (2¾ oz/½ cup) peas, frozen or fresh

S&P

parmesan, to garnish (optional)

Broccoli Pesto

1 broccoli head, trimmed into florets (no stalk)

60 ml (2 fl oz/¼ cup) extra-virgin olive oil

10 g (¼ oz/½ cup) mint leaves

10 g (¼ oz/½ cup) flat-leaf (Italian) parsley leaves

1 garlic clove

zest and juice of 1 lemon

1 teaspoon salt

green chilli, as much or as little as you like (optional)

In a shallow casserole dish or large saucepan, heat the olive oil over a medium heat and add both onions with a big pinch of salt. Fry until the onions begin to soften.

While the onions are cooking, prepare the broccoli for the pesto. Bring a small saucepan of salted water to the boil and blanch the broccoli for 3–4 minutes, or until just cooked. Do not overcook; you want to keep that bright green colour. Drain the broccoli in a colander and run it under cold water until cool. Set aside to drain.

Using the same pot that you used for the broccoli, heat the stock until hot.

Add the garlic to the onions and cook out for a second, then add the rice.

Stir well to coat, then cook over a low heat until the grains begin to look a little translucent around the edges.

Slowly begin to add the warm stock to the rice – about 250 ml (8½ fl oz/1 cup) at a time. Stir, almost constantly, over a low heat until the rice is just cooked through and creamy. If you don't need all the stock, don't use it. Different brands of rice need slightly different amounts of stock, so use your best judgement.

While the risotto is cooking, make the pesto. In a blender or food processor, combine the broccoli with all the pesto ingredients and blend until smooth.

Once the rice is cooked – not mushy, but just cooked (about 25 minutes) – add the peas and allow to cook for a couple of minutes. Remove from the heat and fold in the pesto. Sprinkle with some parmesan, if using, and a good crack of black pepper.

Bolognese

Serves 4–6

Perfectly made bolognese is right up there with freshly washed sheets, new socks or an unwatched season of a good new TV show. And the next best feeling to eating pasta with perfectly made bolognese is having a second batch in your fridge/freezer for another day. Spread it on the base of a pizza or layer it in an epic lasagne (page 105); you can't go wrong. Minimum cooking time is forty-five minutes to one hour. If it's Sunday and you're cleaning the house, just let it simmer away – the longer the better.

INGREDIENTS

80 ml (2½ fl oz/⅓ cup) extra-virgin olive oil

1 brown onion, diced

½ carrot, diced

1 large celery stalk, diced

6–8 button mushrooms, diced

3 garlic cloves, minced

2 tablespoons capers, minced

2 tablespoons caper juice from the jar

½–1 teaspoon chilli flakes (depending on how hot you like it)

1 teaspoon dried oregano

3 tablespoons tomato paste (concentrated purée)

200 g (7 oz/2 cups) vegetable mince or soaked TVP (Textured Vegetable Protein)

250 ml (8½ fl oz/1 cup) unsweetened soy milk (or your favourite milk)

250 ml (8½ fl oz/1 cup) red wine

400 g (14 oz) fresh or tinned diced tomatoes

700 g (1 lb 9 oz) passata (puréed tomatoes)

250 ml (8½ fl oz/1 cup) beef stock

2 teaspoons porcini powder

1 bay leaf

½ bunch of basil, torn

big handful of flat-leaf (Italian) parsley leaves, chopped

S&P

Heat the oil in a large saucepan or high-sided pot over a medium heat. Add the onion, carrot, celery and mushrooms and sprinkle with a big pinch of salt. Fry until soft and beginning to turn a light golden colour.

Stir in the garlic, capers and caper juice, chilli flakes, oregano and tomato paste and cook for another minute, or until the garlic no longer smells raw. Add the vegetable mince and stir until well coated.

Pour in the soy milk and stir, scraping any bits from the bottom of the pan, until it has been almost completely absorbed. Add the wine and simmer until reduced by half, then add all the remaining ingredients except the fresh herbs.

Season to taste with salt and pepper, then stir well and cover with a lid, leaving it slightly ajar. Reduce the heat to low and simmer for 45 minutes to 1 hour, stirring often.

Once cooked, check the sauce. Depending on what tomatoes you have used, you may want to add a little sugar if it's too acidic.

To finish, remove the bay leaf, stir through the basil and parsley, and adjust the seasoning.

DOUBLE BATCH THIS RECIPE AND THANK US LATER.

Carbonara

Serves 4–6

This is the definition of giving people what they want: a heavy, rich cream sauce with bacon. People asked, here it is and oh is it ever delicious. The best way to serve this is to cook the pasta first, then add it to the sauce. To clarify, you're making just enough sauce to coat the pasta you're cooking. Store the rest in the fridge or freezer for a lazy night in front of the TV that calls for a big bowl of creamy pasta. Think ahead, people.

INGREDIENTS

olive oil, for frying

75 g (2¾ oz/½ cup) bacon, diced

cooked spaghetti, to serve

handful of flat-leaf (Italian) parsley, chopped, to garnish

25 g (1 oz/¼ cup) parmesan, to garnish (optional)

Carbonara Sauce

450 g (1 lb/2 cups) red-skinned potato, diced

½ brown onion, chopped

2 garlic cloves, peeled

500 ml (17 fl oz/2 cups) water

125 g (4½ oz/½ cup) butter

70 g (2½ oz/½ cup) cashews, washed and soaked overnight (see Note)

½ tablespoon lemon juice

1 teaspoon black salt (or regular salt)

pinch of ground turmeric

1 teaspoon dijon mustard

250 ml (8½ fl oz/1 cup) unsweetened soy milk

1½ tablespoons nutritional yeast

To make the carbonara sauce, combine the potato, onion and garlic in a large saucepan and pour in enough of the water to cover the veg. Add a big pinch of salt and bring to the boil. Cook until the vegetables are very soft, super mushy and practically overcooked.

Add the remaining sauce ingredients (including any remaining water). Blend the sauce until completely smooth using a regular or hand-held blender. Set aside while you cook the bacon.

Heat a good splash of olive oil in a frying pan over a medium heat and cook the bacon until almost crispy; there's nothing worse than overcooked vegan bacon.

Pour the blended sauce back into a clean saucepan and warm through over a low heat for about 5 minutes to bring all the flavours together. Add the cooked bacon and stir to combine.

Set aside some of the sauce to store for later, then add cooked spaghetti to the remaining sauce – never put the sauce over the spaghetti. Chuck in a handful of parsley and sprinkle with parmesan, if using, to serve.

Note: You can avoid soaking your cashews overnight if you work with broken cashew pieces instead of whole cashews. Just rinse them well and blend.

Thai Jackfruit & Veg Curry

Serves 4–6

Shannon created this dish for a non-vegan chef friend who needed something vegan; Shannon's door is where all desperate, non-vegan chefs come knocking. This is her take on a khao soi curry. The brief for the dish was something that could stand on its own, side by side with a heavily meat-based menu at a heavily meat-based restaurant.

INGREDIENTS

2 tablespoons coconut oil

1 teaspoon curry powder

60 ml (2 fl oz/¼ cup) fish sauce

2 tablespoons soy sauce

1 teaspoon salt

30 g (1 oz) palm sugar (jaggery) or brown sugar

2 x 482 g (1 lb 1 oz) tins green jackfruit, rinsed and pulled apart

400 ml (13½ fl oz) coconut milk

200 ml (7 fl oz) vegetable stock or water

6 kaffir lime leaves

vegetables of your choice, such as zucchini (courgette), carrot, baby corn, potato, snow peas (mangetout), bok choy (pak choy) – whatever's kicking around in your fridge

juice of 1 lime, to garnish

large handful of coriander (cilantro) leaves, to garnish

large handful of Thai basil leaves, to garnish

cooked rice or noodles, to serve

Curry Paste

½ teaspoon fennel seeds

1½ tablespoons coriander seeds

½ teaspoon cumin seeds

2 green cardamom pods, seeds only

8 dried red chillies, soaked (seeds removed for a milder paste)

1 lemongrass stem, white part only

10 g (¼ oz) galangal

10 g (¼ oz) fresh turmeric

150 g (5½ oz) shallot

40 g (1½ oz) garlic cloves (approx. 3 cloves), peeled

20 g (¾ oz) fresh ginger

½ bunch of coriander (cilantro) stalks

1 tablespoon belacan (optional)

To make the curry paste, heat a frying pan over a medium heat and toast the fennel, coriander, cumin and cardamom seeds until fragrant, then blitz to a powder using a high-speed blender or mortar and pestle. Set aside.

Combine all the remaining ingredients in a blender and blitz to a paste. Add a tiny splash of water if needed to loosen the mixture. Add the powdered spices and blitz again until combined.

For the curry, heat the oil in a large saucepan over a medium–low heat, then add 6 tablespoons of the curry paste. Fry for a few minutes, or until it no longer smells raw.

Add the curry powder, fish sauce, soy sauce, salt and palm sugar and cook until the sugar has melted. Toss the jackfruit through the paste and cook for another few minutes, then stir in the coconut milk, stock and kaffir lime leaves.

Add the vegetables of your choice and bring to a gentle simmer. Once the vegetables are cooked, adjust the flavour with lime juice if needed and finish with the coriander and Thai basil.

Serve with rice or noodles.

Scalloped Potatoes

Serves 4–6

Is there anyone out there who grew up without scalloped potatoes? Or even a version of them? Both Shannon and I have really fond/funny memories of our families' scalloped potatoes. Shannon loves her mum's version, but she used to layer the potatoes with tomatoes and that grossed Shannon out. My mom used to make hers from a box with those dehydrated potatoes – and, holy moly, that synthetic sauce and rehydrated potato was next level, and she used to put those French-fried potato strings on top. Potato inception. See: scalloped potato food memories. Now it's time to make your own. And, of course, this one is ridiculous. Honestly, it will barely make it to your plate. We're talking eating it straight from the dish realness here.

INGREDIENTS

250 g (9 oz/1 cup) butter, plus extra to dot on each layer

2 tablespoons minced garlic

1 tablespoon chopped thyme leaves

1 tablespoon chopped rosemary leaves

150 g (5½ oz/1 cup) plain (all-purpose) flour

625 ml (21 fl oz/2½ cups) vegetable or chicken stock

250 ml (8½ fl oz/1 cup) unsweetened soy milk

approx. 1 tablespoon nutritional yeast

approx. 1 kg (2 lb 3 oz) red-skinned potatoes, peeled and thinly sliced (how much depends on the size of your dish)

1 large or 2 small brown onions, halved and thinly sliced

S&P

sweet paprika, for sprinkling

parmesan, to garnish (optional)

Melt the butter in a saucepan over a medium heat and fry the garlic and herbs for 1 minute. Add the flour and cook out for about 2 minutes, but make sure not to colour the roux!

Slowly add the stock, then the soy milk, and whisk until very smooth. Add the nutritional yeast and season with salt and pepper, then cook over a low heat for about 5 minutes. Remove from the heat and set aside.

Preheat the oven to 180°C (350°F).

To build, layer the potatoes and onions with a few dots of butter, some salt and pepper, and the sauce. Repeat until it reaches the top of the heatproof dish, then finish with a sprinkle of sweet paprika and as much parmesan as you like, if using. Bake for 45 minutes to 1 hour.

Spanakopita

Makes 1 large pie or 12 triangles

Ah, the almighty traditional Greek vegetarian dish: so delicious, yet never made vegan. TA-DA!
Another classic made without cheese, but with plenty of flavour. Everyone, but especially Greek
vegans, rejoice! Spanakopita can be made in all shapes and sizes; just make sure to follow the
same instructions and adjust the cooking time.

INGREDIENTS

80 ml (2½ fl oz/⅓ cup) extra-virgin olive oil

1 red onion, sliced

3 garlic cloves, minced

3 spring onions (scallions), sliced

500 g (1 lb 2 oz) silverbeet (Swiss chard) (approx.
  1 small bunch)

zest and juice of 1 lemon

½ teaspoon chilli flakes

½ teaspoon ground cumin

pinch of ground cinnamon

300 g (10½ oz/2 cups) Feta (page 197)

½ bunch of flat-leaf (Italian) parsley, roughly chopped

½ bunch of dill, roughly chopped

parmesan (sort of optional, but it's much better with it)

250 g (9 oz/1 cup) butter, melted

1 box filo pastry

S&P

black and white sesame seeds, to garnish

Heat the oil in a large frying pan over a low heat, add
the onion, garlic and spring onion and allow the mixture
to slowly cook away and lightly caramelise while you
prepare the silverbeet.

To prep the silverbeet, cut the stalks away from
the leaves, then cut the stalks into ½ cm (¼ in)
strips crossways and put them in a colander. Cut the
silverbeet leaves in half lengthways, then cut them into
1 cm (½ in) strips. Rinse well under cold water, as
silverbeet tends to be really dirty.

Dump the silverbeet stalks and leaves into the pan
with the onions. (If it doesn't all fit at once, cook half,
letting it shrink down, then add the rest.) Increase the
heat and allow the liquid to reduce.

Add the lemon juice, chilli flakes, cumin and
cinnamon and season with salt and pepper. Stir well to
make sure everything is coated. Empty the mixture into a
large bowl and leave to cool to room temperature.

When the mixture has cooled, add your feta, but
make sure you've drained away as much oil as possible
or it will be too greasy. (It's even worth lining a small
bowl with paper towel to drain the cheese and using a
slotted spoon to scoop it out.)

Fold the drained feta, the parsley and dill through the
silverbeet mixture and add as much parmesan as you
like, if using. Mix until combined, then set aside.

We use a heatproof baking dish that's approximately
35 x 25 cm (14 x 10 in), but it really doesn't matter; use
a bigger or smaller dish if you prefer. Grease the dish
with some melted butter using a pastry brush.

Preheat the oven to 170°C (340°F).

Cover the base and sides of the dish with filo pastry.
(We suggest two double layers, side by side, so that the
filo overlaps in the middle and over the side.) Repeat
this process, layering butter and filo, until you have
10 sheets on the bottom – that's your bottom layer.
Fill the pastry with your silverbeet mixture, then layer up
another five to ten filo sheets on top. Roll in any excess
pastry from the sides, tucking it in to make a nice folded
edge. Make it as neat or as rustic as you want – there
are no rules here.

To finish, brush the top with melted butter and
scatter over the sesame seeds. Bake for approximately
35–45 minutes, or until the pastry is deliciously golden
and crispy.

Photo page 103.

Caponata Sauce

Makes approx. 1 litre (34 fl oz/4 cups)

Oddly enough for a vegan business, we rarely have eggplant on our menu. It seems too obvious and so many people have had negative eggplant experiences. Plus, it's another 'What do vegans even eat, anyway?' situation ... eggplant? Probably just eggplant. So, when Shannon does cook with it, she uses it very thoughtfully and very well. This sauce, with the combo of kalamatas, chilli and herbs, has quite a lot going on. Like all sauces, it's good to have in your fridge or freezer. Use it on pizza or slather it on crunchy toasted bread with fancy olive oil for a warmed bruschetta vibe. Stir through a bowl of pasta, use it to fill your pies or just eat it straight from the pan. Why not?

We also recommend (though it's completely optional) folding some vegan tuna through this badass sauce. Definitely a best seller when it's in the case at the Deli. The tuna truly makes this sauce the best version you've ever had – vegan or not!

INGREDIENTS

80 ml (2½ fl oz/⅓ cup) extra-virgin olive oil

1 brown onion, diced

1 small red capsicum (bell pepper), diced

1 red bird's eye chilli, finely sliced (seeds removed for a milder sauce)

1 celery stalk, finely sliced

250 g (9 oz/1½ cups) eggplant (aubergine), diced

½ teaspoon dried oregano

1 large garlic clove, minced

2 tablespoons capers

50 g (2 oz/⅓ cup) good-quality pitted black olives (we like kalamatas)

1½ tablespoons red-wine vinegar

1 x 400 g tin best-quality diced or whole tomatoes

handful of flat-leaf (Italian) parsley, roughly chopped

2 thyme sprigs

250 g (9 oz) tuna (optional)

S&P

Heat the oil in a large saucepan or high-sided frying pan over a medium heat and add the onion, capsicum, chilli and celery with a big pinch of salt. Cook for a few minutes until the veg begins to soften.

Add the eggplant and season to taste with salt and pepper. Once everything has softened and started to colour, add the oregano, garlic, capers and olives. Continue cooking until the eggplant has turned a light golden brown. (Add an extra splash of oil if the pan gets too dry; eggplant loves oil.) Don't rush this dish; the whole process up to this point should take about 15 minutes.

Deglaze the pan with the vinegar, then stir in the tomatoes. Once everything is well combined, add the parsley and thyme and mix well. Season with salt and pepper, then reduce the heat to low and simmer for about 20 minutes. If you're using tuna, fold it into the mixture about 10 minutes before the end of the cooking time. Remove the thyme sprigs before serving.

Photo page 102.

CAPONATA

BARLEY, FETA, ZUCCHINI, MINT & LEMON SALAD

TURKISH BRAISED GREEN BEANS

LASAGNE

CREAMY PESTO
POTATO SALAD

SPANAKOPITA

Turkish Braised Green Beans

Serves 4–6 as a side dish

This dish is the definition of ugly delicious; it's nothing to look at and gets passed up every single time we put it in the savoury case at the Deli. But it's the dish our staff collectively hope doesn't sell out so they can all have it for lunch and take home for dinner. Don't be fooled by the look of this one, and definitely forget what you think you know about green beans. These aren't crispy and bright; they are delightfully soggy and muted and pretty much the best thing ever. Great as a side dish eaten at any temperature, but always best eaten with an entire loaf of bread.

INGREDIENTS

80 ml (2½ fl oz/⅓ cup) extra-virgin olive oil

1 large red onion, sliced

3 garlic cloves, minced

½ teaspoon cumin seeds

½ teaspoon chilli flakes

200 g (7 oz/1 cup) fresh or tinned diced tomatoes

500 g (1 lb 2 oz) flat or regular green beans, trimmed and halved if extra long

250 ml (8½ fl oz/1 cup) water or vegetable stock

1½ tablespoons red-wine vinegar

1 teaspoon caster (superfine) sugar

¼ bunch of dill, chopped (feel free to use more; Shannon's obsession with dill means there's often more than ¼ bunch in her green beans, but this is totally personal)

S&P

Heat the oil in a frying pan over a medium heat and fry the onion until it begins to soften. Add the garlic, cumin and chilli flakes and cook for another minute before adding the tomatoes. Cook for a further 5 minutes.

Add the remaining ingredients, except the dill, and reduce the heat to low. Cover the pan with a lid and simmer for 30 minutes, then remove the lid and simmer for another 15 minutes to thicken the sauce slightly.

To finish the dish, stir in the dill and season with salt and pepper.

Photo page 102.

Lasagne

Serves 8

Bold statement: best lasagne you've ever had.
And now that we've gotten that out of the way …

Many of the recipes in this book are interchangeable and have heaps of uses, which by our definition is the sign of a good, useful cookbook. This is one of those recipes. You already have the best lasagne of all time with the bolognese and cheesy béchamel, but add our feta and pesto and you'll blow 'em all away. We had to put a stop to serving this at the Deli because our chefs became full-time lasagne-makers and we never had anything else in the case. Exaggeration – but that's how it felt. This is the definitive recipe to whip out when someone is suspicious of vegan food, or if you're trying to prove a point. It will convince them. We promise.

This recipe feeds eight, but feel free to make a smaller lasagne for one or two people. Refrigerate any leftovers overnight, then you can easily slice it into portions the next day, wrap and freeze.

INGREDIENTS

1 batch Bolognese (page 092)

1 batch Cheesy Béchamel Sauce (page 193)

½ batch Pesto (page 201) or ½ bunch of basil leaves

150 g (5½ oz/1 cup) Feta, drained (page 197)

approx. 8 large lasagne sheets (or 16 small)

50 g (1¾ oz/½ cup) parmesan

Preheat the oven to 170°C (340°F).

Start by quartering your bolognese and cheese sauce, and divide the pesto and feta into thirds.

Evenly coat the bottom of a heatproof dish with some of the bolognese sauce.

Top with the first layer of lasagne sheets. Don't be afraid to overlap, but don't leave gaps. Break the sheets in half if you need to.

For the next layer, top with bolognese, cheese sauce, pesto and crumbled feta. Repeat for another two layers, finishing with an even layer of cheese sauce.

Place the dish on a baking tray (to catch any spills), cover with foil – making sure the foil doesn't touch the surface of the cheese – and bake for 40 minutes, or until the cheese melts, is golden brown and the edges are bubbling. After 30 minutes of baking, remove the foil and sprinkle the parmesan over the top of the lasagne.

Remove from the oven and leave to stand for 15 minutes to cool slightly and firm up before serving.

Photo page 103.

Beef Stroganoff

Serves 4–6

Beef stroganoff was made popular by mothers all around the world as a dinner party staple in the 1980s. It may seem dated, but it's popular for a reason. Stick with the original recipe and serve this on hot buttered pasta or white rice.

The best thing about dishes like beef stroganoff – and using mutton chunks – is that they're real winners with your meat-eating dinner guests who are skeptical about your flavourless vegan lifestyle. Also greatly received by those friends who are really missing the carnivorous childhood favourites their mums and grans used to make.

INGREDIENTS

60 g (2 oz/¼ cup) butter

2 tablespoons olive oil

1 brown onion, sliced

250 g (9 oz) mushrooms (Swiss are best), sliced

1 teaspoon caraway seeds

3 garlic cloves, minced

1 tablespoon smoked paprika

1 tablespoon sweet paprika

1 tablespoon tomato paste (concentrated purée)

250 g (9 oz) beef pieces or mutton chunks

1½ tablespoons plain (all-purpose) flour

500 ml (17 fl oz/2 cups) beef or vegetable stock

1 tablespoon worcestershire sauce

1 tablespoon red-wine vinegar

1 tablespoon wholegrain mustard

125 g (4½ oz/½ cup) sour cream or cream cheese

handful of dill, chopped

S&P

Heat the butter and oil in a large saucepan over a medium heat and fry the onion, mushrooms and caraway seeds until slightly coloured. Add the garlic and cook off for 1 minute, then add the paprikas and tomato paste. Cook for a further minute, then toss in the beef.

Add the flour and cook out for 1 minute before adding the stock, worcestershire sauce, vinegar and mustard. Simmer for about 20 minutes, then stir in the sour cream and dill. Stir over a low heat for about 5 minutes, or until the sour cream has melted. (Don't boil the mixture or the sour cream might split.)

Season to taste.

THIS STROG ALSO MAKES AN EXCELLENT PIE FILLING.

Mac & Cheese Sauce

Serves 4–6

Return of the Mac & Cheese Sauce is a staple take-home meal at the Deli. We like to vary what we put in the cases week to week, but the issue with our mac sauce is that people want it all the time. So it kind of looks like this is your lucky day.

This recipe makes heaps of sauce – much more than your single evening meal – so keep it for the week and use it for cheesy broccoli or nachos, or really on any dish where you need cheese (which should be all of them). The key to making mac and cheese is to boil the amount of pasta you're going to eat and generously fold the sauce through it, saving the rest for later. Add some chipotles, jalapeños, bacon bits – anything to make this recipe your own. For the baked version, undercook the pasta a little bit, fold your sauce through and put it into a casserole dish. Top with breadcrumbs or crushed pita crisps.

One final note: this mac sauce is predominantly made of veg, but don't be fooled; it is not like the veggie nutritional yeast, soup-like mac sauces you'll find online. This is super creamy, cheesy and tasty. Just the way it should be.

INGREDIENTS

450 g (1 lb/2 cups) red-skinned potato, peeled and diced

150 g (5½ oz/½ cup) sweet potato, peeled and diced

1 brown onion, diced

2 teaspoons salt

500 ml (17 fl oz/2 cups) water

375 g (13 oz/3 cups) shredded cheese (we use half cheddar, half parmesan)

125 g (4½ oz/½ cup) butter

70 g (2¾ oz/½ cup) cashews, soaked overnight (see Note on page 095)

4 garlic cloves, peeled

1 tablespoon dijon mustard

2 tablespoons lemon juice (approx. 1 lemon)

1 teaspoon sweet paprika

60 ml (2 fl oz/¼ cup) nutritional yeast

170 ml (5½ fl oz/⅔ cup) unsweetened soy milk

pepper, to taste

Boil the potatoes and onion with the salt and water until very soft and mushy. Transfer the vegetables to a blender and add the remaining ingredients. Blend until very smooth.

Return to a clean saucepan and cook over a low heat until the cheese has melted and the sauce is smooth.

HOT TIP: MAC & CHEESE IS A KILLER PIE FILLING.

Fried Rice

Serves 4–6

In our opinion, fried rice can do no wrong. Food court or fine dining – all fried rices are good.
The keys are not overcooking the rice, and nailing your sauce ratio: not wet and not dry, that's
the perfect fried rice balance. Use this recipe for any and every fried rice variation under the sun,
throw in some vegan egg, vegan ham, or go full traditional and get your peas and cubed carrot
involved. But best of all, follow the kimchi variation in the Note below for one of our personal
favourite Deli take-home meals.

INGREDIENTS

80 ml (2½ fl oz/⅓ cup) vegetable oil

2 garlic cloves, minced

1 teaspoon minced ginger

1 red chilli, sliced

1 carrot, finely diced

½ zucchini (courgette), finely diced

80 g (2¾ oz/½ cup) fresh or frozen peas

2–3 spring onions (scallions)

handful of shredded Chinese cabbage (wombok)

1/3 block smoked tofu, sliced like bacon, or vegan
   bacon

740 g (1 lb 10 oz/4 cups) jasmine rice, cooked and
   cooled

2 tablespoons light soy sauce

2 tablespoons fish sauce

1 tablespoon oyster sauce

1 tablespoon Shaoxing wine or dry sherry

1 tablespoon sesame oil

handful of coriander (cilantro), chopped, to garnish

handful of Thai basil leaves, torn, to garnish

Heat the oil in a large frying pan over a high heat,
then add the garlic, ginger and chilli and fry quickly.
Add all the vegetables and tofu or bacon and fry until
they begin to soften.

Stirring quickly, add the rice and mix until well
combined, then add the sauces, sherry and sesame oil
and toss until well combined. Throw in the coriander and
basil and you're good to go.

*Notes: Leftover steamed rice from last night's take-out
meal is perfectly good to turn into fried rice. Recycling!
Just be careful to toss any rice that's hung around for
too long.*

*Deli favourite kimchi fried rice variation:
add 2 tablespoons gojuchang (Korean chilli paste)
and 80 g (2¾ oz/1 cup) chopped kimchi with its juice
(either home-made, pages 190–1, or store-bought) to
the veg while they're being fried off. Yum!*

Mushroom White Bean Cassoulet

Serves 4–6

Give them all the meat, the French casserole said. Give them pork sausage, confit goose, duck, mutton and pork skin, and add some white beans for good measure. In the south of France, this traditional dish is the definition of carnivorous casserole heaven. However, our version emphasises the white beans and introduces the mushroom (as mushrooms are an ideal meat replacement). Talk about a filling meal. We challenge your relatively skeptical non-vegan friends to walk away from this feeling hungry.

INGREDIENTS

3 tablespoons butter

2 tablespoons vegetable shortening

1 leek, white and light green parts only, halved lengthways and sliced

1 brown onion, roughly diced

1 large carrot, cut into 1.5 cm (½ in) cubes

½ fennel bulb, roughly diced

2 celery stalks, roughly diced

½ celeriac (approx. 500 g/1 lb 2 oz), skin removed, cut into 1.5 cm (½ in) cubes

250 g (9 oz) baby Swiss brown mushrooms, halved (if small, leave them whole)

2 large garlic cloves, minced

1 teaspoon smoked paprika

2 sausages, chopped (optional)

1 teaspoon herbes de Provence

240 g (8½ oz/2 cups) tinned or cooked dried white beans

35 g (1¼ oz/¼ cup) plain (all-purpose) flour

4 thyme sprigs

1 tablespoon sage leaves, chopped

2 bay leaves

125 g (4½ oz/½ cup) passata (puréed tomatoes)

500–750 ml (17–25½ fl oz/2–3 cups) vegetable or chicken stock

handful of flat-leaf (Italian) parsley, chopped

150 g (5½ oz) fresh breadcrumbs (blend up any stale bread you have lying around)

S&P

extra-virgin olive oil, for drizzling

Preheat the oven to 160°C (320°F).

Melt the butter and vegetable shortening in your favourite casserole dish over a medium heat. Fry the leek, onion, carrot, fennel and celery with a big pinch of salt until beginning to soften. Add the celeriac, mushrooms, garlic, paprika and sausage (if using), and season with more salt and pepper. Cook for a few minutes.

Add all the remaining ingredients, except the breadcrumbs and parsley, and add enough stock to cover. Bring to the boil, then reduce the heat and simmer for a few minutes. Cover with a lid, transfer to the oven and bake for 40 minutes.

Remove the lid, give the dish a stir and adjust the seasoning if needed, then stir in the parsley. The sauce should be thick, not watery. If you need to reduce the liquid, return the casserole to the stove and simmer over a medium heat until the sauce is the consistency of gravy (not a broth). Remove the bay leaves and thyme sprigs.

Scatter the surface with breadcrumbs and drizzle with olive oil.

Return to the oven without a lid and continue baking for 15–20 minutes, or until golden and bubbly.

Note: A word on beans: we encourage you to use dried beans as opposed to tinned and to cook them how you like them.

Korean Hotpot
Budae Jigae

Serves 4–6

One bonus amazing thing about Shannon's creativity is that she's a sharer. Anything she loves, she shares with us. Budae Jigae is another example. Most people, especially vegans, have NEVER had this dish. In a land of tofu scrambles and kale Caesars, Shannon goes out of her way to give you flavours you've either never had or never thought you could have.

Budae Jigae is translated as 'Korean army-base stew' and is a perfect example of Korea's newer, hybrid style of cooking. When the Korean army was stationed in Hawaii, Koreans would take food from the US army bases (Spam, hot dogs, Kraft singles and baked beans) and incorporate it into traditional Korean dishes. This is the rough origin of this dish. There's no vegan Spam out there (yet), but there are vegan hot dogs. And if you wanna get traditional, add a tin of baked beans and a slice of cheese. Sounds weird, but somehow it works.

INGREDIENTS

1 litre (34 fl oz/4 cups) vegetable or chicken stock

10 cm (4 in) piece of kombu

2 slices ginger

1 garlic clove, peeled

2 dried shiitake mushrooms

125 ml (4 fl oz/½ cup) kimchi juice

spring onion (scallion) ends (quantity = whatever you have in the fridge)

1 tablespoon *gochugaru* (Korean chilli flakes)

1 tablespoon fish sauce (optional)

1 teaspoon sesame oil

1 tablespoon *gojuchang* (Korean red chilli paste)

1 tablespoon toasted sesame seeds, to garnish

handful of coriander (cilantro), to garnish

cooked rice, to serve

Toppings

vegetables

tofu

noodles

kimchi

herbs

Shannon's favourite toppings: carrot, Asian mixed mushrooms (king oysters, baby oysters, shiitake, enoki), zucchini (courgette), garlic shoots, bean sprouts, spring onions (scallions), leek, kimchi, Korean rice cakes, hot dogs and noodles

Combine the stock, kombu, ginger, garlic, mushrooms, kimchi juice and spring onion ends in a large, shallow saucepan and bring to the boil, then turn off the heat. Strain, discarding the solids, and return the stock to the pot. Add the gochugaru, fish sauce, sesame oil and gojuchang and stir to combine.

Remember, this is a very visual dish and you'll be eating out of the pan you're cooking in. Arrange your choice of vegetables, tofu, noodles and other toppings like a wheel of fortune in the base of the saucepan, but don't put similar colours together.

Carefully pour over the stock and bring to a simmer over a medium–low heat. Simmer gently, for 5–10 minutes, until the noodles and vegetables are cooked. Garnish with the sesame seeds and coriander.

Allow your friends time to take their Instagram photos of the dish before you mix it up. Put your rice and hot pot in the middle of the table and let everyone serve themselves bit by bit. Just make sure they're getting all the delicious components.

Spaghetti Squash & Sausage

Serves 2 as a main or 4–6 as a side dish

For Australians, spaghetti squash is one of those weird veggies that seemingly came out of nowhere. One day it was nowhere to be seen, the next, everyone was making spaghetti out of squash. But really, let's say one thing up front: we're not pretending it's like real spaghetti. If you feel like pasta, make pasta. If you're low-carb and want something yum, make this, but don't be fooled by the word spaghetti.

This is ultimate cold-night food and surprisingly filling to boot. The combo of pesto, creamy wine sauce and sausage is perfection, but it's the strings of spaghetti squash that bring it all together. When you stuff the entire dish back inside the squash shell, cover it in cheese, bake it and eat all of it, it's even more perfect.

INGREDIENTS

1 (smallish) spaghetti squash

60 ml (2 fl oz/¼ cup) extra-virgin olive oil, plus extra for drizzling

½ fennel bulb, diced

1 brown onion, diced

2 sausages of your choice: we prefer crumbled, but feel free to slice it into rounds

2 garlic cloves, minced

½ teaspoon chilli flakes

125 ml (4 fl oz/½ cup) white wine

125 ml (4 fl oz/½ cup) vegetable or chicken stock

2 tablespoons cream cheese

50 g (1¾ oz/½ cup) parmesan, plus extra to garnish

2 tablespoons Pesto (page 201)

60 g (2 oz/1 cup) broccoli or broccolini, cut into florets and blanched

S&P

Preheat the oven to 180°C (350°F).

Cut the squash in half using a large, super-sharp knife and remove all the seeds. Drizzle with olive oil and season well with salt and pepper.

Transfer to a baking tray and roast, cut side up, for about 40 minutes until slightly golden and soft. Remove from the oven and leave to cool. Keep the oven on.

Heat the oil in a shallow casserole dish over a medium heat, then add the fennel, onion and a big pinch of salt and cook for about 5 minutes until softened. Add the sausage, garlic and chilli flakes and cook for about 1 minute, then deglaze the pan with the wine and simmer until reduced by half.

Stir in the stock, cream cheese, parmesan and pesto and cook over a low heat until the cream cheese has melted. Remove from the heat and set aside.

Run a spoon along the inside of the cooled squash halves and remove the flesh. You will see the way the squash runs with the grain. Use a fork to separate the strands. (You can reserve the shells for serving, or just use a heatproof dish.) Return the squash strands to the pan with the sauce, add the broccoli and gently stir to coat, then place the pan back over a low heat for a few minutes.

Transfer the squash mixture to the squash shells or a heatproof dish and sprinkle some extra parmesan on top. Bake for 10 minutes, or until you've achieved a golden crust.

Note: You can use this sauce with or without the spaghetti squash, or use regular spaghetti instead. It also makes a killer pizza topping or scroll filling.

FOR A MOCK-FREE VERSION, SKIP
THE SAUSAGE AND USE EXTRA
BROCCOLI INSTEAD.

Spanish Baked Beans

Serves 4–6

Trust the Spanish chef to take something that is typically bland and English, and turn it into something with pizzazz. This dish is one reason Shannon gets out of bed and, for someone who doesn't eat breakfast, this is big time. Please make these beans a lot; they're hearty, comforting and flavoursome and once you start eating, you won't be able to stop. This is the epitome of moreish. Make sure to serve with plenty of crusty, buttered bread.

INGREDIENTS

480 g (1 lb 1 oz/2 cups) dried Great Northern beans, cooked

1 bay leaf

60 ml (2 fl oz/¼ cup) extra-virgin olive oil

1 brown onion, sliced

½ red capsicum (bell pepper), diced

½ green capsicum (bell pepper), diced

½ fennel bulb, sliced

2 garlic cloves, minced

1 teaspoon thyme leaves

1 teaspoon smoked paprika

½ teaspoon chilli flakes

pinch of saffron threads (optional)

½ teaspoon cumin seeds

2 teaspoons salt

1 tablespoon tomato paste (concentrated purée)

1 tablespoon sherry vinegar

400 g (14 oz) fresh or tinned diced tomatoes

500 ml (17 fl oz/2 cups) vegetable stock or water, or liquid from cooking the beans

1 teaspoon brown sugar

1 tablespoon capers

pepper, to taste

handful of flat-leaf (Italian) parsley, chopped, to garnish

Put the beans in a saucepan and cover with water. Add 1 bay leaf and boil over a high heat until just cooked. Drain the beans and set them aside. Reserve the cooking water.

In another saucepan, heat the olive oil over a medium heat and slowly fry the onion, capsicum and fennel until lightly golden. Add the garlic and thyme and cook for another minute.

Mix in the spices, salt and tomato paste and cook out for a further minute. Deglaze the pan with the vinegar and add the diced tomatoes, stock, brown sugar and capers. Reduce the heat to low and simmer for 30 minutes.

Remove the bay leaf. If you prefer a smooth sauce, purée the mixture in a blender until completely smooth, otherwise just leave it nice and chunky. Add the cooked beans and simmer over a very low heat for 30 minutes to 1 hour. Add a little more stock if needed. Check the seasoning and mix in the parsley to finish.

Twice-Cooked Saffron & Lemon Potatoes

Serves 4–6

This dish is a Spanish and Greek hybrid, and it's a bloody culinary miracle. Just when you thought potatoes couldn't get any better, along came these and they are the best freaking potatoes ever. When Shannon makes these at the Deli, I often wonder if they will make it out the front or just slowly deplete on her workbench. Can't blame her, or any sneaky, potato-thieving staff member, though. I get end-of-the-world defensive as I squirrel away a tiny bowl of these in a secret spot (not telling). They are just as beautiful cold as they are hot, so don't be afraid to treat it like a salad. Final note on these: yum.

INGREDIENTS

500 ml (17 fl oz/2 cups) vegetable or chicken stock

juice of 1 lemon

1 lemon, sliced into rounds

½ brown onion, sliced

2 bay leaves

2 garlic cloves, peeled

3 thyme sprigs

60 ml (2 fl oz/¼ cup) extra-virgin olive oil

1 pinch saffron threads

½ teaspoon dried oregano

1½ teaspoons salt, plus extra for sprinkling

1 kg (2 lb 3 oz) chat (new) potatoes, halved

handful of flat-leaf parsley, chopped, to garnish (optional)

Preheat the oven to 180°C (350°F).

Mix together all the ingredients, except the potatoes and parsley, in a large roasting tin until well combined. (Use a tin that can go from the stove to the oven.)

Add the potatoes and bring to the boil over a medium heat. Cover the tin with foil or a lid, transfer to the oven and bake for 45 minutes. Remove the foil and bake for another 30 minutes, or until most of the liquid has been absorbed and the potatoes are golden.

Check the potatoes from time to time, giving them a bit of a stir to ensure they cook evenly. Finish with a scattering of salt and a handful of chopped parsley, if using.

HEADS UP: THESE SPUDS ARE RIDICULOUSLY DELICIOUS.

Cabbage Rolls

Serves 2 as a main or 4–6 as a side dish

Warning: this traditional Euro recipe is a level up, but don't be scared. This is a perfect rainy-day dish to prepare, as it's got a lot of steps and takes some time – but you can do it! Think about how fancy you'll look turning up to a party with a tray of these gold star–worthy rolls. A word of advice: make your life easier by buying a jar of already cooked and prepared cabbage leaves.

INGREDIENTS

1 large green cabbage, core removed, or 1 jar of pickled cabbage leaves

butter, for dotting over the dish

S&P

sour cream, to garnish (optional)

dill, to garnish (optional)

Filling

440 g (15½ oz/2 cups) white long-grain rice, uncooked

500 ml (17 fl oz/2 cups) vegetable or beef stock

80 ml (2½ fl oz/⅓ cup) extra-virgin olive oil

60 g (2 oz/¼ cup) butter

155 g (5½ oz/1 cup) onion, diced

110 g (4 oz/2 cups) button mushrooms, diced

3 garlic cloves, minced

1 tablespoon chopped thyme leaves

60 g (2 oz/1 cup) dill, chopped

50 g (1¾ oz/1 cup) mint, chopped

1 tablespoon sweet paprika

Sauce

500 g (1 lb 2 oz/2 cups) passata (puréed tomatoes)

500 ml (17 fl oz/2 cups) vegetable stock

80 ml (2½ fl oz/⅓ cup) extra-virgin olive oil

1½ tablespoons caster (superfine) sugar

1 tablespoon red-wine vinegar

Place the cabbage in the biggest pot you have and fill it with enough salted water to cover. Bring to the boil. (The cabbage will float, but don't worry about that.) The cooking time will depend on the size of your cabbage,

but a good indicator is when the leaves start to pull away easily from the cabbage – approximately 30–45 minutes.

Once the cabbage is cooked, remove it from the water, place it in a colander and run it under cold water until it is cool enough to handle. Carefully remove all the leaves, reserving the outer leaves and any torn leaves.

To make the filling, add the rice to the boiling cabbage water and boil until par-cooked. Drain and transfer the rice to a large saucepan with the stock. Bring to the boil, then reduce the heat to low, cover with a lid and cook for approximately 10 minutes, or until the liquid has absorbed. Ensure the rice is still a little undercooked.

Heat the oil and butter in a large saucepan over a medium heat and add all the filling ingredients except the rice. Sauté until soft, then transfer to a large bowl and stir in the rice. Season to taste with salt and pepper and set aside.

Preheat the oven to 170°C (340°F).

Combine all the sauce ingredients in a jug or bowl and set aside.

To make the rolls, pile one-third of a cup of filling onto the core end of each cabbage leaf, then roll them up into mini burritos, ensuring both ends are tucked in and there are no holes for the filling to escape. You should have about 12 rolls. Line a baking dish with the reserved outer and torn cabbage leaves and top with the rolls.

Pour the sauce over the rolls and dot with as much cold butter as you want. Our standard is approximately 60 g (2 oz/¼ cup) butter. Cover the tray with foil and bake for 45 minutes to 1 hour. The foil will trap the heat and help cook the rice and sauce. Remove the foil and bake for a further 15 minutes to allow the sauce to thicken a bit, but not too much – you still want it to look saucy.

Once baked, the rolls can be served hot, cold or at room temperature. Be gentle with the rolls and serve them straight from the dish. Garnish with sour cream and dill, if using.

Egg Salad

Serves 4–6

Oh, look what we did there: gave away a recipe for a sandwich filling. I never thought I'd see the day. Now go forth and prosper – make one million egg and lettuce sandwiches. Or you could turn this into egg and potato salad, add bacon and call it 'breakfast potato salad'. See if we care. It's not the only sandwich filling on the menu, but it is one of the best, and now it's yours to make whenever you want.

Variation: curry your egg salad. Literally just keep adding hot curry powder until you reach your happy place with heat and curry. It's all relative, so no quantities needed.

INGREDIENTS

500 g (1 lb 2 oz) medium/firm tofu (NOT silken or extra firm tofu)

2 celery stalks, finely diced

2 spring onions (scallions), finely sliced

250 g (9 oz/1 cup) Mayonnaise (page 200)

2 tablespoons dijon mustard

1 teaspoon celery seeds

¼ bunch of dill, chopped

¼ bunch of flat-leaf (Italian) parsley, chopped

1 teaspoon black salt

pepper, to taste

First, press the tofu between sheets of paper towel to remove excess moisture; no one likes a sloppy sandwich. To do this, place a couple of paper towels above and below the tofu and sandwich between two plates. Place a heavy can or bag of flour on top and leave to drain while you prepare the veg.

Once drained, mash the tofu in a bowl and add the celery and spring onions. Don't mix it up too much; this is egg salad, not mousse.

Mix all the remaining ingredients in a separate bowl, then add the tofu mixture. Stir well, until the tofu is evenly coated, then refrigerate for at least 1 hour.

NDWICHES
1:30 AM - 4 PM

A $15
ESSED CUBAN: HAM, ROAST TURKEY,
KLES, CHEDDAR + MOJO DRESSING

STEIN $14
I SAUCE WITH FRESH BASIL PESTO, ROCKET
ARELLA ALL TOASTED ON A ROLL

CHES NOT SEALS $14
UB! TURKEY, BACON, LETTUCE, TOMATO,
ON SOURDOUGH

VAMPIRE SLAYER $12
ANCH, SHREDDED ICEBERG, CARROT,
ERY IN A ROLL

LS ME CHICKEN SALAD $12
WITH SHREDDED ICEBERG

WHILE WE TRY OUR BEST,
DELI CANNOT GUARANTEE
ALLERGEN-FREE KITCHEN.

PMA

So
SA

MOREISH PIE FILLINGS

One of our favourite things about this book is its versatility. So many of our ready-meals can be slapped into some delicious Savoury Pie Pastry (page 186) and made into the perfect single-serve meal. We seriously can't think of a dish that couldn't be improved by baking it in our savoury pastry.

Think big: make heaps of filling and pastry and par-cook pies to freeze for those can't-be-bothered nights. You can even freeze the pastry and the fillings separately, ready to make pie decisions later. This chapter includes a few of our favourite pie fillings but, just as our ready meals can be made into pies, these recipes can all be made into main courses and served with mash or rice. And, if you're feeling like mixing it up, you can definitely top these with breadcrumbs or mash as opposed to pastry. We are all about versatility – what can't these meals/pies do?!

Minced Beef Pie

Serves approx. 8 / Makes 1 large, deep-dish pie or 8 small pies

Minced meat pies are as Aussie as they come. And this is the ultimate classic Aussie Four 'n' Twenty minced meat pie. The only difference between these and your service-station favourite is that the main component of these is made from veg. But you'd never know. These would have to be our best-selling Deli item. And it's because EVERYONE loves a minced meat pie. We're talking construction workers, your dad, your best mate, your gran; everyone who comes in — whether they know the food is vegan or not — buys these pies and doesn't question the contents. If you've gotta prove to someone that vegan food doesn't suck, make a batch, smash some sauce on top and don't tell them. They'll never know.

INGREDIENTS

80 ml (2½ fl oz/⅓ cup) extra-virgin olive oil

1 large brown onion, diced

1 carrot, diced

2 celery stalks, diced

2 tablespoons minced garlic

2 tablespoons mushroom powder

1 tablespoon butter

2 tablespoons plain (all-purpose) flour

1 tablespoon tomato paste (concentrated purée)

1 tablespoon thyme leaves

1 teaspoon rosemary leaves

200 g (7 oz/2 cups) TVP (Textured Vegetable Protein), soaked in beef stock

1 tablespoon soy sauce

2 tablespoons worcestershire sauce

125 ml (4 fl oz/½ cup) tomato ketchup

60 g (2 oz/¼ cup) gravy powder

625 ml (21 fl oz/2½ cups) beef stock

1 teaspoon smoked paprika

S&P

Heat the oil in a large saucepan over a medium heat and fry the vegetables, garlic and and mushroom powder until soft. Season with salt and pepper.

Add the butter, flour, tomato paste and herbs and cook for 1 minute before adding the TVP. Stir to coat, then add the remaining ingredients. Reduce the heat to low and simmer for 30 minutes, stirring occasionally. Check and adjust the seasoning if necessary.

As always, allow your mixture to cool before filling the pies.

HOW TO MAKE PIES

To turn any of the fillings in this chapter into an instant meal, just use the same method for constructing a pie given on page 179. Use the Savoury Pie Pastry (page 186) or, if you want a flakier top (like we do at the Deli), you can buy ready-made vegan puff pastry. If you're really pressed for time, you could even buy short or puff pastry from the frozen section at the grocery store (it's often vegan by accident). There's no shame in buying pre-made pastry! Not when you could be eating pies in half the time.

Chicken & Leek Pie

Serves approx. 8 / Makes 1 large, deep-dish pie or 8 small pies

There's something so special about food nostalgia. There's nothing like those dishes that remind you of your nan or your childhood. And even if this pie doesn't evoke that for you, the texture of the flaky pastry with the creamy chicken and veg definitely has that soothing, even-better-than-medicine chicken soup vibe. Especially for those times when you just need food as comfort.

INGREDIENTS

90 g (3 oz/1/3 cup) butter

2 leeks, white part only, halved lengthways then sliced

1 carrot, diced

1 celery stalk, diced

2 garlic cloves, minced

500 g (1 lb 2 oz) chicken, diced (use your favourite brand and keep it fairly chunky)

2 tablespoons chopped thyme leaves

1 tablespoon chopped rosemary leaves

1 tablespoon dijon mustard

50 g (1¾ oz/⅓ cup) plain (all-purpose) flour

125 ml (4 fl oz/½ cup) white wine

250 ml (8½ fl oz/1 cup) vegetable or chicken stock

250 ml (8½ fl oz/1 cup) unsweetened soy milk

1 bay leaf

200 g (7 oz/1 cup) fresh or frozen corn kernels

small handful flat-leaf (Italian) parsley, chopped

S&P

Heat the butter in a frying pan over a medium heat and fry the vegetables and garlic until soft and slightly golden. Add the chicken and cook for another few minutes.

Add the thyme, rosemary, dijon and flour and stir to coat the veg. Cook over a low heat for a few minutes, then pour in the wine and cook off until reduced by half. Slowly add the stock and soy milk, mixing until smooth. Add the bay leaf and simmer over a low heat for 20 minutes. Stir in the corn and parsley, then season.

Remove the bay leaf and allow the mixture to cool completely before filling the pies (see How to Make Pies on page 132).

Thai Curry Chicken

Serves approx. 8 / Makes 1 large, deep-dish pie or 8 small pies

The best bit of this Thai curry chicken recipe is that it's not just for pies. If you can't be bothered with pastry, or need a meal in a pinch, just boil some rice – even instant rice – and pour this bad boy on top. It's one of those voila! recipes. You have a delicious, flavourful meal that makes you look even fancier to your friends. Look, you can make curry! Look, you can make curry that goes into pies! Two meals, one recipe. Voila!

INGREDIENTS

80 ml (2½ fl oz/⅓ cup) vegetable oil

1 carrot, diced

4 spring onions (scallions), sliced

55 g (2 oz/1 cup) button mushrooms, sliced

1 tablespoon minced ginger

2 garlic cloves, minced

2½ tablespoons Thai curry paste (your favourite: red/green/yellow, it's all good)

500 g (1 lb 2 oz) chicken pieces

250 ml (8½ fl oz/1 cup) coconut milk

2 tablespoons fish sauce (optional)

1 litre (34 fl oz/4 cups) chicken stock

125 g (4½ oz/1 cup) green beans, chopped into 1 cm (½ in) pieces

150 g (5½ oz/1 cup) bamboo shoots, chopped (optional)

225 g (8 oz/1 cup) desiree potatoes, peeled and diced

3 kaffir lime leaves, very finely sliced

¼ bunch of coriander (cilantro), chopped

juice of 1 lime

S&P

Heat the oil in a shallow, heatproof casserole dish over a medium heat and fry the carrot, spring onion, mushroom, ginger and garlic until just soft, then stir in the curry paste to coat the veg.

Add the chicken and stir until well coated, then add all the remaining ingredients except the coriander and lime juice. Simmer over a low heat for 15 minutes, then mix in the coriander and lime juice. Season to taste.

For instructions on making your pie, see How to Make Pies on page 132.

Notes: If the sauce seems a little thin, mix 1 tablespoon cornflour (cornstarch) with 2 tablespoons cold water (must be cold), mix well, then stir into the curry until thickened.

If you don't like or can't get your hands on faux chicken, replace it with chickpeas or firm tofu.

Cheesy Broccoli

Serves approx. 8 / Makes 1 large deep-dish pie or 8 small pies

We love cheesy broccoli. Who doesn't? It's that gateway dish that gets little kids (and big kids) interested in vegetables. Hell, add cheese sauce to anything and we'll probably eat it. Fun fact: the cheesy broccoli pie is hands down our most popular veggie-based pie at the Deli. Make this dish with a 50/50 ratio of cauliflower and broccoli, or all cauliflower or all broccoli – whichever will guarantee happiness. And if you're too impatient to make it into pies, or you didn't think ahead and save some pie dough in your freezer, simply put it in a casserole dish and top with breadcrumbs. Instant delicious cheesy veg bake.

INGREDIENTS

2 large broccoli heads (including the tender parts of the stalks), chopped

90 g (3 oz/1/3 cup) butter

80 ml (2½ fl oz/1/3 cup) extra-virgin olive oil

1 large leek, white and light green parts only, halved lengthways then sliced

2 garlic cloves, minced

50 g (1¾ oz/1/3 cup) plain (all-purpose) flour

250 ml (8½ fl oz/1 cup) vegetable or chicken stock

250 ml (8½ fl oz/1 cup) unsweetened soy milk

125 g (4½ oz/1 cup) grated cheese (your choice)

50 g (1¾ oz/½ cup) parmesan (optional)

1 tablespoon nutritional yeast

1 tablespoon dijon mustard

10 g (¼ oz/½ cup) flat-leaf (Italian) parsley, chopped

1 teaspoon chopped thyme

breadcrumbs (optional)

S&P

Bring a saucepan of salted water to the boil and blanch the broccoli until it just begins to soften. Drain and set aside.

Heat the butter and oil in a large saucepan over a medium heat and fry the leek until soft. Add the garlic and cook for 1 minute, then add the flour and cook out for a couple of minutes.

Slowly add the stock and soy milk, and stir until smooth. Mix in the cheeses, nutritional yeast, dijon, parsley and thyme and cook over a low heat until the cheese has melted. Season the sauce with salt and pepper to taste, then add the broccoli. Mix well and continue cooking for another 5 minutes, then remove from the heat and leave to cool completely.

Use as a pie filling (see How to Make Pies on page 132), or top with breadcrumbs and bake straight away.

Shepherd's Pie

Serves approx. 8 / Makes 1 large deep-dish pie or 8 small pies

Cue the chest-beating contest. How funny that, especially in the vegan world, shepherd's pie seems to induce heated debates about whose is the best. Everyone seems to have taken this classic and very typical dish and put their own spin on it. Truthfully, I thought my lentil-based shepherd's pie was the best. That is, of course, until Shannon showed me (and everyone else) up. Talk about typical. Make it. You'll understand.

INGREDIENTS

80 ml (2½ fl oz/⅓ cup) extra-virgin olive oil, plus extra for drizzling

1 brown onion, diced

1 large carrot, diced

2 celery stalks, diced

1 tablespoon minced garlic

110 g (4 oz/1 cup) button mushrooms, diced

1 zucchini (courgette), diced

250 g (9 oz/2½ cups) TVP (Textured Vegetable Protein), soaked, or veggie mince

375 ml (12½ fl oz/1½ cups) beef stock

3 tablespoons tomato ketchup

3 tablespoons BBQ sauce

2 tablespoons Braggs or soy sauce

1 tablespoon balsamic vinegar

2 teaspoons gravy powder

1 teaspoon dijon mustard

1 teaspoon chopped rosemary leaves

1 teaspoon chopped thyme leaves

65 g (2¼ oz/½ cup) fresh or frozen peas

100 g (3½ oz/½ cup) fresh or frozen corn kernels

S&P

sweet paprika, for sprinkling

sprinkling of parmesan, to serve (optional)

Mash

1 kg (2 lb 3 oz) red-skinned potatoes, roughly diced

1 bay leaf

60–90 g (2–3 oz/¼–⅓ cup) butter

extra-virgin olive oil, for mashing (optional)

unsweetened soy milk, for mashing (optional)

S&P

Preheat the oven to 180°C (350°F).

Heat the oil in a large saucepan over a medium heat and add the onion, carrot, celery, garlic, mushrooms and zucchini. Cook until beginning to soften, then add the TVP.

Add all the remaining ingredients, except the peas and corn, and cook over a medium heat for about 20 minutes. Add the peas and corn and season well with salt and pepper.

For the mash, put the potatoes in a large saucepan, add the bay leaf and cover with cold salty water (a small handful of salt will do). Bring to the boil and cook until a knife goes through the potato without resistance. Drain, remove the bay leaf, and mash. Shannon only adds butter, salt and pepper to taste, but feel free to add extra-virgin olive oil or a splash of soy milk as well.

To make individual pies, line the bottom of the pie dishes with pastry. Fill the dishes three-quarters of the way with the filling and top with mash.

If you're making a big traditional shepherd's pie, fill a deep baking dish three-quarters of the way with the meat filling, then top with mashed potato. Drizzle with extra-virgin olive oil, sprinkle with sweet paprika and top with parmesan, if using. Bake until golden and crispy.

Note: To get extra fancy, use a piping (icing) bag with a star-shaped nozzle to pipe your mash on instead, as we have done here.

SUPER YUM

Sweet Case

How do you make a selection of your favourite sweet recipes when you have literally hundreds to choose from? This is by no means an exhaustive list, but simply a few of our favourite things. Some are sentimental, some are obsessions and some are functional. Shannon's aim is to always make things not just good enough for vegans, but good enough full stop. This includes really basic sweets like cookies and cakes. She takes these recipes beyond the usual vegan substitutes – flax, banana, etc. – and investigates how to effectively replace the cream, butter and eggs. And for someone who doesn't care for sweets, she's certainly made a massive impact on every customer who leaves happily carrying their trays of Deli desserty goodness.

Coconut Jam Slice

Makes approx. 9–12, depending on your generosity

Not just for nanas, although she'll be stoked if she's coming around for tea.
You may even become her new favourite grandchild, especially if you use her home-made jam for
this recipe; that's a double whammy! Coconut, biscuit and jam = a definitive recipe for success. This
recipe is the epitome of 'I'll just have one bite. No, maybe just one more bite. This is the last bite,
I swear… '. It'll be gone before you know it.

INGREDIENTS

315 g (11 oz/1 cup) raspberry jam (or any jam you like)

Topping

5 teaspoons No Egg combined with 7 tablespoons water

180 g (6½ oz/2 cups) shredded coconut

80 g (2¾ oz/⅓ cup) caster (superfine) sugar

Base

150 g (5½ oz/1 cup) plain (all-purpose) flour

1 tablespoon cocoa powder

65 g (2 oz/¾ cup) desiccated coconut

125 g (4½ oz/½ cup) butter, melted

115 g (4 oz/½ cup) caster (superfine) sugar

1 teaspoon vanilla

Preheat the oven to 180°C (350°F).

To make the topping, whisk the No Egg and water until frothy and well combined. Mix the coconut and sugar in a bowl and fold in the egg mixture until the coconut is covered and sticky.

For the base, mix together the flour and cocoa in a bowl. Add all the remaining ingredients and combine, using your hands, until the mixture comes together. Press the base mixture into a lined 35 x 25 cm (14 x 10 in) brownie tin (or something similar) and bake for 15–20 minutes until slightly golden.

Remove from the oven and leave to cool for 10 minutes, then spread the jam over the surface and top with the coconut topping. Bake for a further 20–30 minutes until lightly golden brown. Allow to cool completely in the tin before slicing.

Pink Grapefruit & Black Pepper Rectangles

Makes approx. 12–16

Don't be scared by the black pepper. Seriously, we've come this far. Trust us. What an opportune recipe to fully explain Shannon's devout commitment to using savoury ingredients in sweet dishes. In every Smith & Daughters dessert menu and Smith & Deli sweet case there's always a hint of a herb, a salt, an olive oil or a pepper in some form. Perhaps it's her rebellion at having to create desserts when she's far more interested in savoury dishes. Keep in mind, friends, there's only pepper in the base and it does have a very specific function. Bake them, enjoy them, then make your judgement.

INGREDIENTS

Base

225 g (8 oz) butter, at room temperature, plus extra for greasing

80 g (2¾ oz) icing (confectioners') sugar

300 g (10½ oz/2 cups) plain (all-purpose) flour

¼ teaspoon salt

¼–½ teaspoon pepper

Filling

2 tablespoons plain (all-purpose) flour

100 g (3½ oz) cornflour (cornstarch)

450 g (1 lb/2 cups) silken tofu

460 g (1 lb/2 cups) caster (superfine) sugar

3 tablespoons pink grapefruit zest (approx. 1 large grapefruit)

170 ml (5½ fl oz/⅔ cup) pink grapefruit juice (approx. 1 large grapefruit)

Preheat the oven to 170°C (340°F). Grease a 27 × 27 cm (10¾ × 10¾ in) brownie tin and line with baking paper.

For the base, combine the butter and sugar in the bowl of a freestanding electric mixer fitted with the paddle attachment and cream together until pale and fluffy. Add the flour, salt and pepper and beat until it comes together. Press the mixture into the prepared tin and prick the base all over with a fork. Bake for 20 minutes, or until lightly golden, then remove from the oven and set aside to cool. Leave the oven on.

To make the filling, whisk the flour and cornflour together in a bowl, then set aside. Put the tofu in a blender and blend until very smooth, then add the sugar and blend until combined. Add the grapefruit zest and juice and the flour mixture, then blend well.

Pour the filling over the cooled crust, then bake for 35–40 minutes, or until almost set – it should still have a little jiggle in the middle. Cool completely before cutting.

Note: You can also make these into small tarts. Simply cook for 25–30 minutes instead. Just make sure you have the same jiggly centre.

Lemon Tart

Makes 1 large or 4 small tarts

Simply put, this is our favourite lemon tart recipe. Now it's yours. Feel free to take the meringue from the Cherry Meringue Pie (pages 165–7) and make it a lemon meringue pie. If you want to replace the lemon with another citrus, make another citrus happen, especially if something good is in season. And last (but not least), make the tart a bit savoury by adding some thyme or black pepper to the crust. Don't be scared: trust us.

INGREDIENTS

1 quantity Tart Pastry (page 187)

60 g (2 oz) plain (all-purpose) flour

60 g (2 oz/½ cup) cornflour (cornstarch)

450 g (1 lb/2 cups) silken tofu

460 g (1 lb/2 cups) caster (superfine) sugar

60 g (2 oz) lemon zest

170 ml (5½ oz/⅔ cup) lemon juice

Preheat the oven to 170°C (340°F).

Press your pre-made pastry into a greased and lined 25 cm (10 in) round tart tin and prick all over with a fork. Bake for 20 minutes until lightly golden, then remove from the oven and leave to cool.

Whisk together the flour and cornflour in a bowl, then set aside. Put the tofu in a blender and blend until very smooth. Add the sugar and blend until combined, then add the lemon zest and juice, and then the flour mixture. Blend again until well mixed.

Pour the filling over the cooled crust and bake for 30–40 minutes (or 10–20 minutes if you're making small tarts), or until almost set – it should have a little jiggle in the middle. Cool completely before cutting.

Photo page 151.

Scones

Makes approx. 8

For that person who loves pastry but nothing overly sweet, scones are that very simple gateway.
Great for a light brekkie pastry, perfect for tea and, due to the small amount of sugar in these, this
recipe can also be used to make an American-style biscuit (think biscuits and gravy). Serve with
your favourite jam, butter and/or whipped cream (and whatever else you want). These scones
are also great for making a quick strawberry shortcake. Simply cut in half and layer with whipped
cream and fresh strawberries, 'cause why not?

INGREDIENTS

500 ml (17 fl oz/2 cups) unsweetened almond or
soy milk

1 tablespoon lemon juice

60 g (2 oz/¼ cup) butter, melted, plus extra for brushing

2 teaspoons No Egg combined with 2 tablespoons
cold water

600 g (1 lb 5 oz/4 cups) plain (all-purpose) flour,
plus extra for dusting

1½ tablespoons baking powder

1 teaspoon bicarbonate of soda (baking soda)

1½ tablespoons caster (superfine) sugar

1 teaspoon salt

Preheat the oven to 200°C (400°F).

Mix the soy milk, lemon juice and melted butter in a
small jug or bowl. Add the egg mixture and set aside for a
few minutes to allow the milk to thicken.

Sift the flour, baking powder and bicarb soda into a
mixing bowl, then stir in the sugar and salt. Add the wet
ingredients to the dry and mix with your hands until only
just combined. Don't overwork it or you'll have rock-hard
scones. The dough will feel quite soft and sticky, but
that's how it's meant to be. If it's too sticky, just add 35 g
(1¼ oz/¼ cup) flour to help bring it together.

Tip the dough onto a floured surface. Use your hands
(not a rolling pin) to lightly flatten and roll out the dough
until it's 3 cm (1¼ in) thick. Cover with a tea towel (dish
towel) and leave to sit for 10 minutes.

Using an 8 cm (3¼ in) round cutter (or whatever cutter
you have) dipped in flour, cut out your scones. If you don't
have a cutter, don't run to the store. Get an empty tin
can, give it a rinse and use that. When pressing out the
scones, don't twist the cutter – just push down and pull
up. This saves it from sealing the sides of the dough and
will ensure you get flaky, textured sides.

Transfer the scones to a baking tray lined with baking
paper and position them about 1 cm (½ in) apart. Brush
the tops with melted butter and bake for 12–15 minutes,
until golden.

Photo page 150.

SCONES

LEMON TART

Brownies

Makes approx. 12

We did the maths. We've made nearly 150 types of brownies since we opened our doors in June 2015. With a new flavour each week, our pastry elves work mega hard to come up with new flavour combos. No recipes, no guidebooks: just pure, spontaneous, fun decision-making. The base stays the same, but the flavour always changes. Sometimes it's a bit crazy, but sometimes people like crazy. And people definitely LOVE brownies. And we especially love that these cater for our gluten-free friends. Rejoice! There's something nice and baked for you!

INGREDIENTS

185 g (6½ oz/¾ cup) butter

125 g (4½ oz/½ cup) plain yoghurt

1½ teaspoons vanilla

345 g (12 oz/1½ cups) light brown sugar

225 g (8 oz/1½ cups) gluten-free flour

90 g (3 oz/¾ cup) cocoa powder

1 teaspoon baking powder

¼ teaspoon bicarbonate of soda (baking soda)

250 ml (8½ fl oz/1 cup) unsweetened soy milk

175 g (6 oz/1 cup) chocolate chips

Preheat the oven to 170°C (340°F).

Combine the butter, yoghurt, vanilla and brown sugar in the bowl of a freestanding electric mixer fitted with the paddle attachment and cream for about 3 minutes until very light and fluffy.

In a separate bowl, mix together the flour, cocoa, baking powder and bicarb soda. Add to the butter mixture and slowly beat until well combined. Slowly pour in the soy milk, while still beating, until fully combined.

Fold in the chocolate chips, then pour the batter into a greased 27 × 27 cm (10¾ × 10¾ in) brownie tin. Bake for approximately 45 minutes. Keep an eye on it, as it may take a little less or more time. Your brownies should still be a little jiggly in the middle. Cool completely in the tin before turning out and slicing.

Note: Go wild folding different fillings into your brownie dough, such as jam or Caramel Sauce (page 210). Just make sure to only add wet ingredients to the dough. Go even wilder and add any toppings you like: Chocolate Sauce (page 211), Buttercream (page 199), crushed-up cookies, marshmallows, nuts, etc.

Passionfruit Shortbread Sandwich Cookies with Raspberry Buttercream

Makes approx. 16 cookies or 8 sandwich cookies

We call this the photogenic publisher's-choice cookie. These little beauties were in the sweet case the day our lighting tests were done, and they were so gosh darn beautiful in the test shots that we had to include them in the book (what show-offs). Jokes aside, this is one of the many brilliant variations of our sandwich cookies that we proudly display week in and out. They're not your traditional Aussie melting moment (or yo-yo); these are punchier, with better shortbread and a brilliant buttercream filling. Don't be fooled – the use of two fruits doesn't make these healthy. But they are delicious. And they're pink!

INGREDIENTS

170 g (6 oz) butter, softened, plus extra for greasing

100 g (3½ oz) icing (confectioners') sugar

50 g (1¾ oz) passionfruit pulp

1 teaspoon vanilla

300 g (10½ oz/2 cups) plain (all-purpose) flour, plus extra for dusting

pinch of salt

Buttercream

30 g (1 oz/¼ cup) frozen raspberries, thawed and extra liquid drained

250 g (9 oz/1 cup) butter

625 g (1 lb 6 oz/5 cups) icing (confectioners') sugar

1–2 drops natural red food colouring (optional)

To make the cookie dough, mix the butter and icing sugar in a bowl until smooth and well combined. Add the passionfruit pulp and vanilla and mix well.

In another bowl, whisk the flour and salt until combined. Add the passionfruit mixture to the flour and rub with your fingers until well incorporated. Wrap the dough in plastic wrap and leave to rest in the fridge for about 30 minutes.

Preheat the oven to 170°C (340°F).

On a lightly floured surface, roll out the cookie dough to about 3–4 mm (⅛ in) thick. Using a 4 cm (1½ in) round cookie cutter, cut out the cookies and place them on a baking tray lined with baking paper. Transfer to the oven and bake for 10–15 minutes, or until the edges of the cookies start to turn golden. Allow to cool completely before filling with the buttercream.

To make the buttercream, combine the raspberries and butter in the bowl of a freestanding electric mixer fitted with the whisk attachment and beat until just combined. With the mixer at low speed, gradually add the icing sugar, 120 g (4½ oz/1 cup) at a time, until it has all been incorporated. Continue beating on medium speed for about 2 minutes. At this point, you can add food colouring if you would like a stronger pink colour.

Fill a piping (icing) bag with the buttercream and pipe some filling onto the flat side of a cookie. Sandwich with another cookie, flat-side down, and continue until all the cookies have been filled. Alternatively, simply spread the buttercream on the cookies with a knife.

Choc Chip Rosemary Cookies

Makes 10

By far, this is the most beloved Deli cookie, even over the snickerdoodles, gingerbread friends and every variety of sandwich cookie. So that says a lot. We thought the savoury elements (salt, olive oil and rosemary) might put our customers off, but it was quite the opposite. People are rightfully obsessed with these. Word to the wise, this is Shannon's favourite cookie – BUT she will only eat these if they're warm, so follow the chef's advice on that one. Get 'em while they're hot. It's always a 'sad' day when one of these takes a tumble off the rack and straight into our hands. Can't serve that to a customer …

INGREDIENTS

270 g (9½ oz) light brown sugar

150 g (5½ oz) butter, softened

1 teaspoon vanilla

1 teaspoon No Egg combined with 3 tablespoons water

2 teaspoons extra-virgin olive oil

260 g (9 oz/1¾ cups) plain (all-purpose) flour

1 teaspoon baking powder

¼ teaspoon salt, plus extra for sprinkling (use the fancy sea salt flakes on top if you've got 'em)

1 teaspoon chopped rosemary leaves

150 g (5½ oz) chocolate chips

Preheat the oven to 170°C (340°F).

We prefer to mix these cookies manually in a bowl so they don't get overworked, but feel free to use a freestanding electric mixer. Just be careful not to over-cream the butter and sugar, as this will affect how the cookies spread out.

Using a wooden spoon, cream the brown sugar, butter and vanilla in a mixing bowl until fluffy, but not too fluffy. If using a mixer, make sure you use the paddle attachment and mix until well combined and lightly creamed.

In another bowl, whisk together the No Egg mixture and oil until frothy and well combined. Pour the egg mixture into the creamed sugar and stir to combine, then add the flour, baking powder and salt. Mix until the flour is completely combined, then fold in the rosemary and chocolate chips.

Roll your cookies into ten even-sized balls and transfer to a baking tray lined with baking paper, ensuring they are evenly spaced to allow room for spreading. This recipe makes ten 90 g (3 oz) cookies, but you can roll them into whatever size you like.

Bake for 15–25 minutes, depending on how soft you like your cookies. If you like them fudgy (aka the best way to eat them), go with 15 minutes; if you like crispy then go for 25 minutes. Sprinkle with salt.

Best eaten straight from the oven while still warm. The cookies are perfectly fudgy if they hold their shape but are still soft.

Photo page 158.

CHOC CHIP
ROSEMARY
COOKIES

Maple Sandwich Cookies

Makes approx. 12

Our most popular cookies are always filled cookies, no matter what, which makes me think we have the smartest customers in the world. Why have one cookie when you could have two, and with a bonus layer of icing in between them? They're so smart. Plus, it's simply our job to look for opportunities to maximise the deliciousness of every transaction. For us, it's simple maths but also simple construction: take the first piece, apply a delicious adhesive, affix the second piece = maximum efficiency.

Our flavours always outdo themselves. Maybe it's the North American in me, but these maple numbers are a personal favourite. Not just available in Canada, we say! Don't put them too close to me or you may never see them again.

INGREDIENTS

125 g (4½ oz/½ cup) butter

55 g (2 oz/¼ cup, firmly packed) brown sugar

¼ teaspoon salt

1 teaspoon baking powder

1 teaspoon vanilla

½ teaspoon ground ginger

½ teaspoon mixed spice

4 tablespoons maple syrup

185 g (6½ oz/1¼ cups) plain (all-purpose) flour, plus extra for dusting

Filling

50 g (1¾ oz/¼ cup) Copha or vegetable shortening, softened to room temperature

125 g (4½ oz/½ cup) butter

½ teaspoon vanilla

¼ teaspoon maple extract

2 tablespoons maple syrup

250 g (9 oz/2 cups) icing (confectioners') sugar

pinch of salt

Preheat the oven to 180°C (350°F).

To make the cookies, beat together all ingredients, except the maple syrup and flour, in a bowl until fluffy. Stir in the maple syrup, then fold in the flour.

Press the dough into a ball and roll out on a floured surface to about ½ cm (¼ in) thick. Using a maple leaf cutter (or any cutter you have), cut out the cookies and place on a baking sheet lined with baking paper. Bake for 10–12 minutes, or until they are lightly browned on the edges. Remove from the oven and leave to cool completely on a wire rack.

We don't recommend mixing the filling by hand. Instead, combine the Copha and butter in the bowl of a freestanding electric mixer fitted with the paddle attachment and beat for 2 minutes, or until super light and fluffy. Reduce the speed to low and, with the motor running, add the vanilla, maple extract and maple syrup. Gradually add the icing sugar and salt and beat until well combined and fluffy.

Place a teaspoon of the filling onto the flat side of a cookie. Top with another cookie, flat-side down. Repeat until all the cookies are filled. Refrigerate for at least 30 minutes before serving to allow the filling to firm up.

Photo page 159.

Banana Split Cake

Serves 8–12

Upon arrival, our customers make a beeline for our sweets case. What flavour doughnut or vanilla slice or cookie is on display today? But there's a special happiness reserved for the Banana Split Cake. Is it the cherry on top? Is it the sprinkles? Or is it just that people know how ridiculously delicious our banana cake is?

This cake is extremely versatile, so don't feel you have to go all out with the toppings. You can make exceptional banana bread or banana muffins using this recipe (sans fun toppings): just pour the cake batter into a loaf (bar) tin or a muffin tin. This recipe also lends itself to many great additions, so mix in a handful of your favourite ingredients: choc chips, toasted walnuts, raspberries, chopped vegan bacon – anything! And no need to alter the recipe to accommodate these extra ingredients.

INGREDIENTS

125 g (4½ oz/½ cup) butter

345 g (12 oz/1½ cups) caster (superfine) sugar

1 teaspoon vanilla

3 ripe bananas, mashed

170 ml (5½ fl oz/⅔ cup) unsweetened soy milk

1 teaspoon bicarbonate of soda (baking soda)

pinch of salt

½ teaspoon ground cinnamon

335 g (12 oz/2¼ cups) plain (all-purpose) flour

Egg Mixture

1 teaspoon Vegg

4 teaspoons No Egg combined with 80 ml
  (2½ fl oz/⅓ cup) water

Toppings

cherries, crushed peanuts and sprinkles, to decorate
  (or whatever you like)

1 quantity Buttercream (page 199) (optional)

1 quantity Chocolate Sauce (page 211) (optional)

Preheat the oven to 170°C (340°F).

To make the egg mixture, whisk the Vegg and No Egg mixture together until frothy and well mixed. Set aside.

Cream the butter and sugar in a mixing bowl until pale and fluffy, then add the egg mixture and vanilla. Mix well. The mixture may curdle at this stage, but that's OK.

Add the mashed banana and mix until combined, then stir in the soy milk, bicarb soda, salt, cinnamon and flour.

If you're making a cake, pour the batter into a 23 cm (9 in) round cake tin, or feel free to use any tin you like. Bake for 45–50 minutes, or until a skewer inserted in the middle of the cake comes out clean. While the cake bakes, prepare your toppings.

Remove the cake from the oven and leave to cool in the tin for 10 minutes before turning out onto a wire rack. Leave to cool completely before decorating.

Top your cake with whatever makes you happy: the sprinkles and buttercream? Go for it. Follow the photo, or create your own chocolate sauce-to-cherry-to-buttercream ratio.

Note: If you can't get your hands on Vegg, up the No Egg by ½ teaspoon and the water by 1 tablespoon.

Photo page 162.

BANANA SPLIT CAKE MAKES PEOPLE SMILE.

BANANA
SPLIT CAKE

Cherry Meringue Pie

Makes 1 large or 4 small pies

This recipe is a tribute to the gal who always makes our pastry cases the best of the best. Our beloved pastry chef and queen of sugar, El, consistently ensures Shannon's every pastry dream is executed to perfection, no matter how crazy Shannon's ideas seem. All bow down to the little guy with the biggest feet.

This recipe is an El special. When asked to contribute one recipe for the book, this is the one she chose. She loves cherries, pies, meringue and blow torches, and this recipe uses all of them! We're pretty happy she chose it; this pie is magnificent.

At the Deli, any time we top something with meringue it just flies out the door. Aquafaba is probably one of the most talked-about surprise vegan baking/cocktail-making/cooking ingredients. It was a serious game changer in vegan food. We've come up with a super-simple meringue recipe for all your vegan meringue needs. Go ahead and use this to top everything: doughnuts, cakes, puddings – everything. The one thing we will say is that it's worth it to go to a hardware store or cooking supply store to get yourself a little blow torch. They're cheap, super fun and surprisingly handy.

One more thing – reserve the cherry juice for making the Laura Palmer on page 214 and, once you've drained the liquid from the chickpeas for the Aquafaba, save the chickpeas for a salad or curry.
Waste not, want not.

Cherry Meringue Pie (continued)

INGREDIENTS

Base

450 g (1 lb/3 cups) plain (all-purpose) flour, plus extra for dusting

250 g (9 oz/1 cup) butter

55 g (2 oz/¼ cup) caster (superfine) sugar

185 ml (6 fl oz/¾ cup) dairy-free milk of your choice

Filling

1 kg (2 lb 3 oz/5 cups) jarred morello or sour cherries, drained (juice reserved)

575 g (1 lb 4 oz/2½ cups, firmly packed) light brown sugar

zest of ½ lemon

2 tablespoons cornflour (cornstarch), sifted

1 tablespoon ground cinnamon

2 teaspoons mixed spice

Meringue

125 ml (4 fl oz/½ cup) Aquafaba

pinch of citric acid

230 g (8 oz/1 cup) caster (superfine) sugar

To make the pie base, combine all the ingredients, except the milk, in a bowl. Using your fingers, rub the butter into the dry ingredients until it resembles loose, wet sand. Make a well in the centre and pour in the milk. Gently incorporate the milk into the flour until you have a firm dough, but be careful not to overwork it. Wrap the dough in plastic wrap and refrigerate for at least 30 minutes.

Once the pastry has had time to rest, grease a 20 cm (8 in) pie dish with cooking spray or some butter. Lightly dust a surface with flour and roll out the pastry to about 4 mm (⅛ in) thick, ensuring it is larger than the tart tin. Gently roll the pastry back over your rolling pin, then unroll it over the top of the pie dish. Use your fingers to gently press the pastry into the dish. Carefully trim any excess pastry with a small knife. Refrigerate for another 30 minutes.

Preheat the oven to 160°C (320°F).

Line the pastry with a piece of baking paper, ensuring it comes up the sides, and fill with baking beads or dried legumes, such as chickpeas or lentils. Blind-bake for 20 minutes, then remove from the oven and leave to cool slightly before removing the baking weights and baking paper. Leave the oven on.

To make the filling, place the cherries and 460 g (1 lb/2 cups) of the brown sugar in a mixing bowl and stir until the cherries are well coated in the sugar. Leave to stand for 30 minutes.

A lot of liquid will have seeped out of the cherries, so use a fine-mesh sieve to drain the excess liquid, then return the cherries to the bowl. Add the remaining brown sugar, the lemon zest, cornflour and spices to the cherries and toss well to mix. Pour into the pastry case and bake for 30–40 minutes (or 15–25 minutes if you're making small pies), or until the filling is bubbling and has noticeably thickened. Remove from the oven and set aside until cool enough to handle.

Gently lift the pie out of the dish and place on a wire rack. (Don't wait until the pie has completely cooled to remove it from the tin, as any bubbled-over filling can harden, causing the pastry to stick.) Leave to cool completely before topping with meringue.

While the pie is cooling, prepare the meringue. Combine the Aquafaba and citric acid in the bowl of a freestanding electric mixer fitted with the whisk attachment. On medium–high speed, whisk the mixture to stiff peaks (be patient, it will take a few minutes). Reduce the speed to medium and slowly add the sugar, 1 tablespoon at a time, whisking constantly. Once all the sugar has been incorporated, increase the speed to high and whisk for a further 3 minutes, or until the meringue is thick and glossy.

Use a spatula to gently spread the meringue on top of the cooled pie and toast the meringue with a blow torch until golden brown all over (don't worry if parts turn black). Make sure you hold the torch about 20 cm (8 in) away from the pie.

Serve immediately!

Thanks El, for making cherry meringue pies that dreams are made of. And for making Smith & Deli a better, sweeter place to be.

Chocolate, Mandarin & Cherry Self-Saucing Pudding

Makes 1 large or 4 small puddings

There's something you should know about Shannon: she hates the commonly beloved combo of chocolate and orange. However, she loves mandarins and even created this recipe, which mixes them with chocolate. Now, it may seem like there's no big difference between mandarins and oranges, but there 100% is. So, if you too are a hater of chocolate and orange, don't skip past this recipe. If you're not like Shannon and love the choc-orange thing, feel free to just use oranges instead. Serve the puddings hot. You can also put them in the fridge, microwave them the next day and they'll still be super yum. In fact, even if you eat them cold, they have a fudgy brownie texture, which is delicious.

INGREDIENTS

300 g (10½ oz/2 cups) plain (all-purpose) flour

4 teaspoons baking powder

50 g (1¾ oz) cocoa powder

225 g (8 oz) light brown sugar

generous pinch of salt

4 teaspoons No Egg combined with 80 ml (2½ fl oz/⅓ cup) water

200 ml (7 fl oz) unsweetened soy milk

160 g (5½ oz) butter, melted, plus extra for greasing

zest and juice of 2 large mandarins

300 g (10½ oz) chocolate chips, melted

200 g (7 oz/1 cup) jarred or fresh pitted sour cherries, drained (reserve the juice for making the Laura Palmer, page 214)

50 ml (1¾ fl oz) Cointreau

500 ml (17 fl oz/2 cups) boiling water

whipped cream or vanilla ice cream, to serve

Preheat the oven to 180°C (350°F).

Mix together the flour, baking powder, half the cocoa, half the brown sugar and the salt in a mixing bowl.

In another bowl, whisk the No Egg mixture, milk, melted butter and mandarin zest and juice. Add the wet ingredients to the flour mixture and stir until combined. Fold in the melted chocolate and cherries.

Either divide the mixture between four individual greased ramekins or pour it all into a round 25 cm (10 in) baking dish. Make sure to only fill the dishes three-quarters of the way so there is still room to pour the liquid over the top.

In a jug, whisk together the Cointreau, remaining cocoa, remaining brown sugar and the water. Stir until the cocoa and sugar have dissolved, then gently pour the liquid evenly over the puddings.

Bake for approximately 15 minutes for smaller puddings or approximately 30 minutes for one large pudding. It's ready when it bounces back when pushed with a fingertip. Serve hot, topped with whipped cream or vanilla ice cream.

Doughnuts

Makes 8–10

If you know the Deli, these doughnuts don't need any introduction. You know it, I know it; they are THE BEST. We have customers who won't even go to the pastry case, but just come straight to the register and order their usual: coffee and a doughnut. I've tried asking them, 'Don't you want to know the flavour today?' (We change them every day.) But they always reply with some variation of, 'Nope, I know it's going to be good, no matter what'. And no matter how wacky the flavours sometimes get, the customer is well and truly right – they're always good.

Direct quote from Shannon about her doughnuts: 'I'm not one to toot my own horn, but tooooot bitches!' Shannon also doesn't usually get high on her own supply, but every Saturday morning, when there are cinnamon cardamom sugar doughnut holes to be had with a coffee, she's never happier.

This doughnut recipe works for all doughnuts: filled, glazed, sugar – anything.

INGREDIENTS

1½ teaspoon dried yeast

145 g (5 oz/⅔ cup) caster (superfine) sugar, plus a pinch for the yeast

125 ml (4 fl oz/½ cup) warm water

550 g (1 lb 3 oz/3⅔ cups) plain (all-purpose) flour, plus extra for dusting

pinch of salt

2 teaspoons No Egg

250 ml (8½ fl oz/1 cup) warm unsweetened soy milk (not hot!)

zest of 1 lemon

4 tablespoons butter

cooking spray

vegetable oil, for deep-frying

cinnamon sugar for dusting, Doughnut Glazes (pages 174–5), or your favourite doughnut topping

Mix the yeast, a pinch of sugar and the warm water in a small bowl and stir to combine. Allow to sit for 5 minutes, or until the mixture is bubbly.

Combine the flour, salt, caster sugar and No Egg in the bowl of a freestanding electric mixer fitted with the dough hook attachment.

In another bowl, mix the yeast mixture with the warm soy milk and lemon zest, then slowly pour it into the mixer on low speed. Continue mixing until the liquid is completely incorporated. If the mixture seems too sticky, add a little extra flour, a tablespoon at a time, until the dough begins to pull away from the side of the bowl.

Add 2 tablespoons of butter to the dough, increase the speed to medium and mix for 1 minute before adding the remaining butter. At this stage, the dough may look as though the butter isn't incorporating. That's OK. If necessary, add a little extra flour, a tablespoon at a time, until the dough begins to pull away from the side of the bowl again. Beat on medium speed for about 4 minutes, or until the dough is soft, smooth and elastic.

Transfer the dough to an oiled bowl and cover with plastic wrap. Set aside to prove in a warm place until doubled in size. This could take anywhere between 30 and 60 minutes depending on the temperature of the room.

FILLING SUGGESTIONS

JAM

CUSTARD

CREAM

ANYTHING YOU WANT

Dust your work surface with flour and dump the dough on top. Dust a rolling pin with flour and roll out the dough until it is approximately 1.5 cm (½ in) thick.

Using two ring cutters, one large and one extra small, cut out your doughnuts using the large cutter, then use the small cutter to cut the doughnut holes. Keep the doughnut holes – chef's treat. If you plan to make filled doughnuts, only use the large ring cutter to cut out discs.

Transfer the doughnuts to a baking tray sprayed with cooking spray. Cover loosely with plastic wrap and allow to prove again until the doughnuts have doubled in size. The dough should feel very soft and bounce back slowly when pressed with a fingertip.

In a deep-fryer or large, heavy-based saucepan, heat enough oil for deep-frying until it reaches 170°C (340°F) on a cooking thermometer, or until a scrap of dough dropped into the oil browns in 15 seconds. Carefully drop a few doughnuts into the oil, making sure not to overcrowd the pan. Fry the doughnuts for approximately 1 minute before turning over and frying for another minute on the other side. Obviously, if you decide to make larger doughnuts, the cooking time will be a little longer, so just go by the colour and make sure the doughnuts are a beautiful golden brown on both sides. Test one by breaking it in half to make sure they are cooked all the way through. Transfer to paper towels and allow to drain and cool slightly.

This is the point where you can get creative and glaze the doughnuts however you like. If glazing, you want the doughnuts to be cold. If dusting in cinnamon sugar, toss the doughnuts in the sugar as soon as they are no longer wet with oil.

If you're making filled doughnuts, fill a piping (icing) bag with whatever filling you choose, then jam a hole in the side of the doughnut with the tip of the nozzle. Jiggle around to make some space, then squeeze in the filling.

Doughnut Glazes

Makes enough glaze for 10–12 doughnuts

Not all doughnuts are created equal, and glaze vs sugar is a divisive topic. So do what makes you happy. The following glazes are for those who like it a bit sweeter, a bit more … fun, if you will. We've given you four different recipes, but feel free to get buck wild on the glazes and definitely don't hold back on your toppings. That's not the point of a doughnut, is it?

Blueberry, Lemon & Thyme

310 g (11 oz/2 cups) frozen blueberries (or other frozen berries of your choice)
zest of 1 lemon and juice of ½ lemon
750 g (1 lb 11 oz/6 cups) icing (confectioners') sugar
1 teaspoon chopped thyme leaves

Microwave the berries on high for 2 minutes, or until defrosted and bubbling. If you don't have a microwave, just leave the berries in a bowl to defrost completely before making the glaze.

Drain off half the liquid and blend or mash until smooth. Add the remaining ingredients and whisk well.

Cover the bowl with plastic wrap to prevent a crust from forming and refrigerate for 15 minutes before glazing. Stir well before use.

Strawberry

310 g (11 oz/2 cups) frozen strawberries
750 g (1 lb 11 oz/6 cups) icing (confectioners') sugar
1 teaspoon vanilla
zest of 1 lemon

Microwave the berries on high for 2 minutes, or until defrosted and bubbling. If you don't have a microwave, just leave the berries in a bowl to defrost completely before making the glaze.

Drain off half the liquid and blend or mash until smooth. Add the remaining ingredients and whisk well.

Cover the bowl with plastic wrap to prevent a skin from from forming and refrigerate for 15 minutes before glazing. Stir well before use.

Chocolate

500 g (1 lb 2 oz/4 cups) icing (confectioner's) sugar

90 g (3 oz/¾ cup) cocoa powder, sifted

pinch of salt

1 teaspoon vanilla

170 ml (5½ fl oz/⅔ cup) non-dairy milk of your choice

Combine all the dry ingredients in a bowl, make a well in the middle and pour in the vanilla and milk. Whisk until smooth.

Cover the bowl with plastic wrap to prevent a skin forming if not using immediately. Stir well before use.

Passionfruit

375 ml (12½ fl oz/1½ cups) passionfruit pulp (seeds sieved out, 2 tablespoons reserved for later)

750 g (1 lb 11 oz/6 cups) icing (confectioners') sugar

zest of 1 lime

Put the strained pulp in a bowl and whisk in the remaining ingredients. Fold in the reserved passionfruit seeds.

FOR MAXIMUM GLAZE EFFECTIVENESS, ALWAYS LEAVE YOUR DOUGHNUTS TO COOL COMPLETELY FIRST.

Honey Cake

Serves 8–12

As an honorary Jew, Shannon was invited to crash Friday night Shabbat dinners and participate in holidays with her Jewish friends growing up. During these dinners and holidays, Shannon took every opportunity to learn about traditional Jewish dishes. One of those was honey cake: a traditional cake for Rosh Hashanah, or Jewish New Year. Lekach, or honey cake, is meant to ensure a sweet new year to come, and having a vegan version means we can have a sweet new year all year round.

This cake is affectionately called the ugly duckling of cakes in our kitchen. If you want to make a pretty birthday cake, this isn't the one. However, it is BIG, understated, delicious and gets better with age. Make it, let it cool, then wrap in plastic wrap and leave to sit for a day (if you can even wait that long). It's similar to a dense, thick gingerbread cake. Just trust us, if Shannon is excited about cake (the gal who doesn't want cake on her birthday, or ever really), trust her. Make it.

This cake is even better when cut and dipped in melted chocolate.
If you would prefer to make two smaller cakes, simply divide the mixture between two
23 x 13 x 7 cm (9 x 5 x 2¾ in) loaf (bar) tins and reduce the baking time by half.

INGREDIENTS

230 g (8 oz/1 cup) caster (superfine) sugar

235 g (8½ oz/⅔ cup) date honey or date molasses (found in Middle Eastern food stores)

235 g (8½ oz/⅔ cup) light agave syrup

160 g (5½ oz/⅔ cup) butter, plus extra for greasing

3 teaspoons No Egg combined with 100 ml (3½ fl oz) water

125 ml (4 fl oz/½ cup) unsweetened soy milk

3 tablespoons rum (whatever rum you've got)

125 ml (4 fl oz/½ cup) coffee

1 teaspoon vanilla

600 g (1 lb 5 oz/4 cups) plain (all-purpose) flour

2 teaspoons baking powder

1½ teaspoons bicarbonate of soda (baking soda)

½ teaspoon salt

3 teaspoons mixed spice

½ teaspoon ground cardamom

½ teaspoon ground ginger

Preheat the oven to 170°C (340°F).

Combine the caster sugar, date honey, agave and butter in a saucepan over a medium heat and cook, stirring occasionally, until the sugar has melted.

Add the No Egg mixture and soy milk to the honey mixture, then add the rum, coffee and vanilla and mix well.

Mix together all of the dry ingredients in the bowl of a freestanding electric mixer fitted with the paddle attachment. With the motor running on medium speed, slowly pour in the honey mixture and mix for about 1 minute.

Grease a 23 cm (9 in) round cake tin. Pour in the cake mixture and bake for 1 hour to 1 hour 10 minutes, checking regularly. It is ready when a skewer inserted in the middle of the cake comes out clean. If the cake begins to get too dark, cover with foil.

Peach & Raspberry Pie

Makes 1 large or 4 small pies

It's always pie time in our house. The Deli may not always have pies on display but, believe us, there's always time for pie. Winter or not. Peach or not. Pie is pie is pie and we always have time for it. If you have heaps of fruit, don't eat it all: save some and make a pie. Hot pie, cold pie, it's all good with us. The fruits in this recipe are interchangeable. Peel apples instead of peaches, and only blanch stone fruits with skin that needs to come off. Another popular Deli variation is making hand pies instead of big or mini pies. Instructions below. What's that? It's pie time, gotta go.

INGREDIENTS

6 large peaches, white or yellow

200 g (7 oz) raspberries (approx. 1 punnet)

170 g (6 oz/¾ cup) caster (superfine) sugar

50 g (1¾ oz/⅓ cup) plain (all-purpose) flour

zest of 1 lemon

1 quantity Sweet Pie Pastry (page 187)

cooking spray, for greasing

1 tablespoon butter, melted

60 ml (2 fl oz/¼ cup) unsweetened soy milk

1 tablespoon raw (demerara) sugar

Bring a saucepan of water to the boil over a high heat. Cut a shallow 'X' on the bottom of each peach and drop them, two at a time, into the boiling water and blanch for 30 seconds. Once the skin starts peeling away from the 'X', remove the peaches using a slotted spoon and immediately drop them into a bowl of iced water.

Once the peaches are cool, remove the skins, cut them in half and remove the pits. Cut each half into approximately six wedges. Combine the cut peaches with the raspberries, sugar, flour and lemon zest in a bowl and stir well to coat the fruit. Set aside.

Preheat the oven to 190°C (375°F).

Divide your pastry into two pieces: one two-thirds and one one-third. Shape the pastry in rough circles and roll out the larger piece on a floured surface to ½ cm (¼ in) thick, making sure it is bigger than the pie dish.

Spray a pie dish with cooking spray. Lay the larger piece of pastry over the dish and gently push it into the corners, leaving pastry hanging over the sides. Fill the pastry case with the fruit mixture, leaving behind any juice collected in the bowl.

Roll the smaller piece of pastry out to a similar thickness as the base, making sure it is large enough to cover the pie. Use a pastry brush or your fingertips to dab some water around the edge of the pie, then top the fruit with the pie lid. Press down gently to secure the two pieces of pastry, then trim any excess using a sharp knife. Using your thumbs or a fork, push down the edges of the pastry to seal the pie and give it a nice finish.

Mix together the butter and soy milk in a small bowl and brush the top of the pie with it. Sprinkle with the raw sugar and cut a small V shape in the pie lid with a sharp knife. Place the pie on a baking sheet, which will catch any overflow and help cook the bottom of the pie.

Bake for 15 minutes, then reduce the heat to 160°C (320°F) and bake for a further 30–40 minutes until golden brown.

Note: To make hand pies like we do at the Deli, roll out the whole quantity of pastry and cut out discs using a small plate. Put your fruit on one half of the disc (leaving some room around the edge), run water along the edge, then fold the pastry over to make a half-moon shape. Follow the remaining steps in the recipe, then bake your pies at 175°C (345°F) for 25–35 minutes until golden.

Simple PASTRY & DOUGH

Shannon's nature prevents her from wanting to measure and write down and follow rules when it comes to cooking. She's the first person to say that getting out scales is one of the most draining things you can do. But, when it comes to breads and doughs, there's something almost cathartic about the process: the precision, feel and time it takes. Before you continue, Shannon would like to declare that she's by no means a baker and this book just touches on a subject that deserves a book of its own. But the one thing she does know is that it's wrong to make pastries or doughs in a rush. Allow yourself the time it takes and just enjoy it. It's especially therapeutic in this age, where people choose convenience over quality.

A note on our pastries and doughs: one thing we hear constantly, particularly about our pies, is how damn good the pastry is. Keep that in mind! Plus, all of these doughs should be considered basics to keep in your freezer so you can make fresh savoury or sweet pies at a moment's notice.

Dill Pretzels with Wholegrain Mustard Butter

Makes 4 large pretzels or 12 smaller ones

In America, particularly New York, you can get a soft pretzel on most street corners. They're as ubiquitous as those molten hot pies at an Aussie service station. Soft pretzels aren't much of a thing in Australia, but they certainly are at the Deli. They're perfectly salty and served with delicious wholegrain mustard butter (most definitely a step up from plain yellow mustard). And they're just so, so, so, so moreish. You won't want to stop at one. Good thing this recipe makes up to 12, hey?

You can still make pretzels by hand without a freestanding electric mixer, but it's a lot of effort. If you do, cancel your gym appointment for the day. Your trainer may frown upon the amount of carbs you've eaten, but they'll be impressed by your arm workout.

INGREDIENTS

200 ml (7 fl oz) unsweetened soy milk

20 g (¾ oz) butter

7 g (¼ oz) dried yeast

2 tablespoons light brown sugar

300 g (10½ oz/2 cups) plain (all-purpose) flour

1 teaspoon salt, plus extra to garnish

1 tablespoon chopped dill

2 tablespoons bicarbonate of soda (baking soda)

1 litre (34 fl oz/4 cups) boiling water

Wholegrain Mustard Butter

125 g (4½ oz/½ cup) softened butter, at room temperature (not melted)

3 tablespoons wholegrain mustard

1 teaspoon salt

Combine the milk and butter and warm to blood temperature (when it feels neither hot nor cold when you put your finger in), either in a bowl in the microwave or in a saucepan on the stove.

Add the yeast and sugar to the milk mixture and leave to sit for 5–10 minutes, or until frothy.

Combine the flour and salt in the bowl of a freestanding electric mixer fitted with the dough hook attachment. Add the dill and the warm milk mixture.

Knead for about 5 minutes until smooth. Cover and leave to prove in a warm place for about 1 hour, or until doubled in size.

While the dough is proving, make your wholegrain mustard butter. Combine all the ingredients in the bowl of a freestanding electric mixer fitted with the whisk attachment and whisk until light and fluffy. You can also whisk the butter by hand.

Knock back the dough and leave it to prove for another 15 minutes. Knock back again, then divide the dough into 12 pieces, or 4 if you're making the big boys. Roll the pieces into ropes and shape into pretzels.

Preheat the oven to 200°C (400°F).

Next, make a bicarb soda solution. In a big, shallow bowl/pan/tray (anything large enough to lie the pretzel in flat), mix the bicarb soda with the water and stir until the bicarb has dissolved.

Dip your pretzel into the solution until fully submerged. If you can't dunk it in all the way, submerge one side, then flip it over and submerge the other. Place on a baking tray lined with baking paper and sprinkle generously with salt. Leave to prove in a warm place for 15 minutes, then bake for 15–20 minutes. Generously slather with or dip in the mustard butter.

Note: It would behove you to get your hands on fancy sea salt flakes or coarse sea salt, particularly for sprinkling these pretzels.

USE THIS WHOLEGRAIN MUSTARD BUTTER ON SANDWICHES OR TOAST — YUM!

Vegemite Cheesy Scrolls

Makes approx. 6–9 scrolls or heaps of tiny, party-sized scrolls

The Vegemite cheesy scroll is to an Aussie kid what the peanut butter and jelly sandwich is to an American kid. In fact, you'd be hard pressed to find someone who has grown up in Australia who didn't have it weekly, in their lunchbox or after school. As someone who was born and raised in the United States and hugely, unusually loves Vegemite (much to the disgust of my fellow Americans), I use these scrolls as ambassadors for the strong, yeasty spread. There's something about adding cheese and dough that puts Vegemite on a whole other playing field. The scroll makes Vegemite approachable and delicious and savoury in a totally different way. Funny story: we once had a customer say the scrolls were too cheesy. We kindly showed them the door.

INGREDIENTS

2 teaspoons dried yeast

2 tablespoons caster (superfine) sugar

375 ml (13 oz/1½ cups) warm water

525 g (1 lb 3 oz/3½ cups) plain (all-purpose) flour, plus extra for dusting

2 teaspoons salt

90 ml (3 fl oz) extra-virgin olive oil

125 g (4½ oz/½ cup) Vegemite, mixed with 2 tablespoons water (the water is key, as it prevents the dough from tearing when spreading the Vegemite)

250 g (9 oz/2 cups) grated cheese of your choice (cheddar, mozzarella, or a mix of all the cheeses)

60 g (2 oz/¼ cup) butter, melted

In a bowl, combine the yeast and sugar with the water and leave for 5 minutes, or until frothy.

Combine the flour and salt in the bowl of a freestanding electric mixer fitted with the dough hook attachment.

Once the yeast is ready, add the oil to the flour mixture. Then, with the motor running slowly, add the yeast mixture. Knead for at least 5 minutes, or until very soft and elastic. If the dough seems too sticky, add a little more flour. Cover and leave to prove in a warm place for 30 minutes, or until doubled in size, then knock back the dough.

Preheat the oven to 190°C (375°F).

Dust a work surface with flour and roll the dough into a rectangle approximately 45 x 30 cm (18 x 12 in). Spread the Vegemite over the dough, then sprinkle with cheese. Roll up the dough like a Swiss roll, then cut into scrolls approximately 8 cm (3¼ in) wide, or just cut into whatever size you want.

Place the scrolls on a baking tray lined with baking paper (suggested: a 45 x 30 cm/18 x 12 in tray), cover with plastic wrap and leave to prove for 20 minutes. Drizzle with melted butter, then bake for 15–20 minutes. Allow to cool for 10 minutes before removing from the tray. Pull apart or use a knife to cut.

Note: There are countless variations on this recipe, but here are some of the bestsellers at the Deli:

• *Kimchi, gochujang (Korean chilli paste) and cheese*

• *Pizza*

• *BBQ ham and cheese*

• *Pesto and cheese*

Pizza Dough

Makes 4 pizza bases

Let's lay down the facts. The best thing about making your own pizza dough is being able to have pizza now AND pizza later. Hot tip: make the whole quantity and store some for later. This recipe makes four good-sized pizza bases, because if you're putting in the effort why stop at two?

Roll out your dough to the desired thickness, sprinkle your pan with polenta or semolina, cover your base in Red Sauce (page 207) and bake at 200°C (400°F) until almost cooked. Leave to cool, stack between pieces of baking paper, wrap tightly with plastic wrap and freeze. Another tip is to slow-prove your dough in the fridge overnight. Remove the dough from the fridge one hour before using to allow it to come to room temperature, then proceed. Look at you go!

---

7 g (¼ oz) caster (superfine) sugar

7 g (¼ oz) dried yeast

300 ml (10 fl oz) warm water

500 g (1 lb 2 oz/3⅓ cups) plain (all-purpose) flour

1 teaspoon salt

1 tablespoon extra-virgin olive oil

Mix the sugar and yeast with the water in a bowl and leave for 5–10 minutes, or until frothy.

Combine the flour and salt in the bowl of a freestanding electric mixer fitted with the dough hook attachment, then pour in the yeast mixture and oil. Knead for about 5 minutes, or until smooth and elastic.

Spray a large bowl with cooking spray or wipe with olive oil. Shape the dough into a smooth ball, put it in the bowl and cover with plastic wrap. Leave to prove in a warm place for about 1 hour, or until doubled in size.

Make pizza.

Savoury Pie Pastry

Makes 1 large pie or 4 small pies

This is another great one for planning ahead and making your life easier. Cook smart. If you have this dough in your freezer, it means savoury pies are never far from your guts. This recipe, though simple, has been perfected at the Deli with our daily offering of pies, and truly makes the best buttery, flaky pastry. Please use for all savoury pies, quiches, tarts – anything that you can wrap in pastry, you probably should.

---

450 g (1 lb/2½ cups) plain (all-purpose) flour

1 teaspoon salt

220 g (8 oz) butter

110 g (4 oz) ice-cold water

Mix the flour and salt in a large mixing bowl. Break the butter into small pieces and rub it into the dry ingredients until well combined. The mixture should resemble wet sand.

Make a well in the middle and pour in the water. Mix until the pastry comes together into a ball with no lumps. Wrap in plastic wrap and chill for at least 30 minutes before use.

Tart Pastry

Makes 1 large pie or 4 small pies

This tart pastry (and all pastries for that matter) is a weapon for your kitchen's back pocket. It's perfectly buttery, super short and not too sweet. Freeze it in batches for your future tarty needs. It really, truly resembles the real deal, so use it.

---

550 g (1 lb 3 oz) plain (all-purpose) flour

50 g (1¾ oz) caster (superfine) sugar

220 g (8 oz) butter

185 ml (6 fl oz/¾ cup) unsweetened soy milk

Combine the flour and sugar in a large mixing bowl and stir to combine.

Break the butter into small pieces, then rub it into the dry ingredients until well combined. The mixture should resemble wet sand.

Make a well in the middle and pour in the soy milk. Mix well until the pastry comes together into a ball with no lumps. Wrap in plastic wrap and chill for at least 30 minutes before use.

Sweet Pie Pastry

Makes 1 large pie or 4 small pies

Use this heavenly pastry for your most classic sweet pies. We swear by it. Any time you want to make a sweet treat and need some pastry, we got you. It might not seem like there's much difference between this recipe and our Tart Pastry (left), but they are two different recipes. Freeze batches of this pastry for when a pie craving hits and you just gots to have it.

---

550 g (1 lb 3 oz) plain (all-purpose) flour

2 tablespoons caster (superfine) sugar

1 teaspoon salt

220 g (8 oz) butter

185 ml (6 fl oz/¾ cup) ice-cold water

Combine the flour, sugar and salt in a large mixing bowl. Break the butter into small pieces, then rub it into the dry ingredients until well combined. The mixture should resemble wet sand.

Make a well in the middle and pour in the water. Mix well until the pastry comes together into a ball with no lumps. Wrap in plastic wrap and chill for at least 30 minutes before use.

EASY BASICS

These are the things you should always have in your fridge/freezer. It's just that simple. We want you to be equipped for any and everything that comes your way. If there was an end-of-civilisation scenario, we're not quite sure how you'd go without electricity or gas, but you'd be stocked with some pretty badass meals and pre-made deliciousness to work with, even if that meant cooking over a campfire. Plus, having these basics on hand makes you look really, really good when you have a spontaneous guest over, or someone is snooping in your fridge. The effort is evident!

Kimchi

Makes approx. 1 kg (2 lb 3 oz) (depending on the size of the cabbage)

If we were to perform an intervention with Shannon, it would be over her insatiable obsession with kimchi. But then again, if we did that, we wouldn't get all the kimchi creations, so we encourage it. Put it on our pizza, in our scrolls, pasta, pies, tacos, salads, soups – everything. Kimchi the world.

Speaking of which, here's a recipe for kimchi paste, so you can literally kimchi anything you want. As an FYI, 'kimchi' is a method. Use this paste as a base and, if you find cheap cucumbers, kimchi them! Pineapple, all types of radish, carrot, spring onion (scallion), lotus root, celery, garlic shoots, raw potato – kimchi it all. Like soup, this is a great recipe for using up what's left over in your fridge. Grab a book on how to do it from your Korean grocer, as times and methods vary when kimchi-ing different fruits and veg.

Very important: *gochugaru* (Korean red chilli flakes) and the belacan ball (dried shrimp paste) are items that can't, and shouldn't, be substituted with anything else. The thing that separates kimchi from all other pickles is the salted seafood: that great funkiness. If you make it sans the belacan, you're just making spicy pickled cabbage. Go to the effort of visiting your Asian grocer and seek out that vegan belacan ball.

INGREDIENTS

40 g (1½ oz) belacan

5 large garlic cloves, peeled

40 g (1½ oz) ginger, peeled and roughly chopped

½ brown onion, roughly chopped

500 ml (17 fl oz/2 cups) water

160 g (5½ oz/2 cups) *gochugaru* (Korean red chilli flakes)

80 ml (2½ fl oz/⅓ cup) fish sauce

1 Chinese cabbage (wombok)

35 g (1¼ oz/¼ cup) good-quality salt

1 bunch of spring onions (scallions), cut into 1 cm (½ in) pieces

You will need one large jar or several small jars, cleaned and sterilised. The easiest way to do this is to run the jars through a hot dishwasher or boil them in water for a couple of minutes before drying them out completely in an oven on a low heat.

To make the paste, blend the belacan, garlic, ginger, onion and water until smooth. Stir in the gochugaru and fish sauce. Set aside.

Trim the end off the cabbage and cut into quarters lengthways. Remove the core from each piece, then cut crossways into 4 cm (1½ in) strips and place in a large bowl. Sprinkle the salt over the cabbage and massage it in, making sure it's well coated. The cabbage will begin to soften. Cover with cold water and use a plate that fits inside the bowl to press down on the cabbage so it is fully submerged. Leave to soak and soften for 1 hour, then drain and rinse well to remove the salt. Return the rinsed cabbage to a clean bowl and mix in the spring onion.

If there's ever a time to wear gloves, it's now. Add your kimchi paste to the bowl and mix really well, running your fingers through the cabbage until it is thoroughly coated. Pack the kimchi tightly into the jar(s). Every time

K.R.E.A.M

KIMCHI RULES EVERYTHING AROUND ME!

you add a handful of cabbage, pack it down, being careful to remove any air bubbles. Leave a 3 cm (1¼ in) gap at the top of the jar, then seal tightly with a lid and leave to ferment in a cool, dark place such as a pantry shelf (not in the fridge).

The kimchi will take 2–5 days to ferment. After 2 days, taste the kimchi. If you prefer it stronger, leave it for the full 5 days. Less will be milder, so give it a taste every day. Once you're happy with the flavour, store the jars in the fridge (chilling slows down the fermentation process). This kimchi will last for weeks – that is, if you can resist the urge to keep eating it.

Basic Couscous

Serves 4–6 as a side dish

Remember couscous? We wish you'd never forgotten this amazing staple. Have this on hand. We have given you a whole book of amazing meals that are super versatile, refrigeratable and freezable. Add this staple and you can meal-plan like the boss you are. Roast a tray of veg, mix it with couscous and you have the simplest meal of all time. Or serve couscous with any of the meals in the take-home section and your dinner is complete. This humble ingredient is also a good base for a salad. Just add some veg, douse it in your favourite dressing and you're done.

Amp it up: add some nuts, herbs, dried fruit, roasted veg or any other ingredient of your choice at the end. How cool is couscous?

INGREDIENTS

2 tablespoons extra-virgin olive oil

2 tablespoons butter

½ brown onion, diced

1 garlic clove, minced

½ teaspoon cumin seeds

300 ml (10 fl oz) vegetable or chicken stock

1 teaspoon salt

200 g (7 oz) dried couscous

pepper, to taste

Heat the oil and 1 tablespoon butter in a saucepan over a medium heat. Add the onion and fry slowly until golden, then add the garlic and cumin seeds and cook for 1 minute.

Pour in the stock and salt and bring to the boil, then remove from the heat and stir in the couscous. Mix well, then cover the pan and leave to sit for 3 minutes. Remove the lid, add the extra tablespoon of butter and fluff up the couscous with a fork. Cover with a tea towel (dish towel) and allow to steam for 5 minutes before serving. Season with pepper.

Cheesy Béchamel Sauce

Makes approx. 1.5 litres (51 fl oz/6 cups)

Consider this the cheesy holy grail recipe with a million uses. This is your sauce for lasagne, cheesy bakes, making cheesy cauliflower. Everything. Chuck it in with whatever you want. If baked mac and cheese is your thing, use this sauce instead of the one on page 111, top with garlicky breadcrumbs and bake 'til bubbly. Or go extra trashy and crush up your favourite cheese puff-esque Cheezels/Cheetos to use as breadcrumbs. All of a sudden, with this up your sleeve, everyone wants to come over for dinner. Give the people what they want – CHEESE!

INGREDIENTS

1 litre (34 fl oz/4 cups) unsweetened soy milk

375 ml (12½ fl oz/1½ cups) vegetable stock

½ brown onion, halved through the root to keep intact

2 garlic cloves, peeled and smashed with the side of a knife

1 bay leaf

4 whole black peppercorns

2 thyme sprigs

125 g (4½ oz/½ cup) butter

110 g (4 oz/¾ cup) plain (all-purpose) flour

1 tablespoon dijon mustard

40 g (1½ oz/¼ cup) nutritional yeast

125 g (4½ oz/1 cup) of your favourite vegan shredded cheese

50 g (1¾ oz/½ cup) parmesan (optional)

S&P

Combine the milk, stock, onion, garlic, bay leaf, peppercorns and thyme in a saucepan and bring to the boil. Remove from the heat and leave to infuse for 10–30 minutes. The longer you leave it, the better it will be. Once infused, strain the milk through a fine-mesh sieve into a jug or bowl, discarding the solids. Set aside.

Heat the butter in a saucepan over a medium heat and whisk in the flour. Cook out for about 2 minutes, keeping in mind that you don't want it to change colour. We're not talking brown here, but barely golden. Slowly add the milk mixture to the roux, whisking continuously until smooth.

Add the remaining ingredients and cook over a low heat until the cheese has melted. Season to taste.

Note: Use this recipe for Lasagne (page 105) and on pizza.

MOST COMMONLY ASKED QUESTION: HOW DO YOU MAKE EVERYTHING SO CHEESY?

ANSWER: THIS SAUCE.

Rice Paper Bacon

Makes 20–30 slices

Through the years there have been a lot of vegan bacons, for the most part all equally inedible. Nowadays, companies are really nailing it with some of the soy bacons currently on the market. When rice paper bacon came along and people could make it themselves at home, we knew we had to try it. Shannon, being queen of the marinades, didn't find it hard to come up with something truly delicious. Her version, while not being as eerily similar to bacon as some of the soy, gluten and mushroom mock-meats, has the perfect crunch and is great for crumbling onto salads or using in sandwiches.

A word about working with rice paper. If you can get your hands on square rice paper, grab it. It will produce more consistently-shaped bacon. If you have round rice paper and don't trim the rounded bits off, then you will have curled edges. If that doesn't bother you, then no worries. Here, Shannon has trimmed her circles into squares. For each rice paper circle you will get four 5 cm (2 in) pieces of bacon.

The marinade will make up to 20–30 slices of bacon. It will keep in the fridge, so make as much or as little as you want and store the rest for another day.

INGREDIENTS

10 rice paper sheets

Bacon Marinade

3 tablespoons Maggi Original seasoning sauce

½ tablespoon kecap manis (Indonesian sweet soy sauce)

1 teaspoon liquid smoke

2 tablespoons vegetable oil

½ teaspoon Spanish smoked paprika

1 teaspoon maple syrup

½ teaspoon worcestershire sauce

½ teaspoon salt

½ teaspoon tomato paste (concentrated purée)

Combine all the marinade ingredients in a large bowl or shallow tray, such as a roasting tin. You need something big enough to accommodate your rice paper.

Fill another bowl or roasting tin with cold water.

Take two sheets of rice paper and line them up, then use scissors to cut your bacon into strips. You can use a knife, but you won't get the same clean lines.

Hold two of the strips back to back and immerse in the cold water for 10 seconds. Rub the sheets between your fingers while submerged to ensure the water gets in between the strips.

Once they become a little soft, take them out of the water. They should stick together. Try to line the strips up as closely as possible. If they're not exact, don't stress. If they fall apart, you'll have to put them back in the water for another couple of minutes to seal. Just don't over-soak them or they'll get too soft. Treat it like a pancake: the first one may be a bit crap, but you'll get it.

Line a baking tray with baking paper and preheat the oven to 170°C (340°F).

Give your marinade a quick stir, then pass the rice paper strips through it until completely covered. Lift them out and allow any excess to drip off. The goal is for the rice paper to not be too wet; you're not drying them

WE KNOW. THIS ISN'T ACTUALLY BACON, BUT IT'S REAL TASTY.

out, just getting rid of the excess. Lay them out on the baking tray. Repeat with as many strips as will fit on the tray, arranging them as close as possible without touching. Bake for 5–10 minutes, depending on your oven.

Check the strips after 3–4 minutes. Once they crisp up, flip them over to crisp the other side. Once cooked, remove from the oven and leave to cool completely.

Store the strips in an airtight container. Make a batch for the week and crumble them over salads or chuck them in your sandwiches.

Note: Before baking the strips, keep in mind that people love bacon-wrapped food. And this bacon can be wrapped around things. It will cook faster than the thing you're wrapping, so give your chicken fillet – or whatever – a head start, then wrap in bacon right at the end of the cooking time.

Feta

Makes 500 g (1 lb 2 oz)

Before you make your mind up about tofu actually becoming feta, just stick with us. The trick is giving it enough time for the flavours to develop and overthrow the tofu flavour. If you use this straight away, it will most definitely taste like tofu with flavour added. However, leave it overnight and watch what happens. It is a very good idea to always have a jar of this in the fridge. Just make sure to keep it covered in olive oil and properly sealed.

Preferably, make feta one day before you need it. It can then be used with many of our recipes: Lasagne (page 105), Greek Watermelon Salad (page 044), Spanakopita (page 100) and a million other dishes. And it would be remiss of us not to mention that this feta would be perfect on Melbourne's (un)official dish, avocado on toast. You may not be able to afford a house, but you can afford this feta. Avocado is another story.

INGREDIENTS

500 g (1 lb 2 oz) firm tofu, crumbled into feta-style bits (be careful not to crumble too small)

250 ml (8½ fl oz/1 cup) extra-virgin olive oil

250 ml (8½ fl oz/1 cup) vegetable oil

125 ml (4 fl oz/½ cup) red-wine vinegar

2 teaspoons salt

1 teaspoon dried oregano

1 teaspoon caster (superfine) sugar

½ teaspoon chilli flakes

1 garlic clove, minced

¼ red onion, thinly sliced

plenty of pepper

First, press the tofu between sheets of paper towel to remove excess moisture. To do this, place a couple of paper towels above and below the tofu and sandwich between two plates. Place something heavy, like can or bag of flour, on top and leave to drain.

Combine all the ingredients, except the tofu, in a large bowl. Once the tofu has drained, mix it in and leave to marinate at room temperature for at least 6 hours.

Soy Yoghurt

Makes approx. 500 g (1 lb 2 oz/2 cups)

While pre-made, store-bought yoghurt substitutes are evolving and the selection is ever-expanding, we're still a bit limited by what is readily available in stores. Most vegan yoghurts have a strong coconut flavour because they're usually coconut-based. Even the neutral, non-sweetened, non-vanilla flavoured yoghurts have a very strong coconut flavour. These are awesome for brekkie, desserts and dishes that work with coconut, such as curries, but sometimes you just need a neutral-flavoured yoghurt, and this is the recipe for you. It's super easy once you get the hang of it, so don't be scared. Think of how cost effective – and crafty – it will be to make your own, and how satisfied you'll feel knowing what's in your yoghurt.

INGREDIENTS

50 g (1¾ oz/⅓ cup) cashews

500 ml (17 fl oz/2 cups) unsweetened soy milk

1½ tablespoons store-bought natural, unsweetened yoghurt of your choice

pinch of salt

Combine the cashews and soy milk in a blender and blend until very smooth. Pour into a small saucepan and warm over a low heat until the mixture reaches blood temperature (when it feels neither hot nor cold when you put your finger in). Stir in the yoghurt and salt.

Leave to sit in a warm place for at least 8 hours. Once you've reached your desired yoghurtyness, transfer to the fridge to stop the culture growing. It will keep in the fridge for up to 2 weeks.

Note: It may seem odd using store-bought yoghurt to make yoghurt, but you need existing cultures to make more. You need the living thing that makes yoghurt what it is. The bit of pre-bought yoghurt is just the starter. You can certainly use probiotic capsules, but it's cheaper to buy pre-made. After you make the first batch, you can use your home-made yoghurt to make four to five batches of future yoghurt before you have to buy pre-made again.

Buttercream

Makes approx. 900 g (2 lb/6 cups) buttercream (enough to ice 1 large cake or 6 small cakes)

We don't know why the 'challenge' of vegan buttercream puts off so many pastry chefs. But here we have it, and it's the best one we've developed so far. Use this as a base buttercream and add lemon zest, cocoa powder, food colouring or extract, such as mint or almond. Just be careful when adding the liquid – too much and it will make the buttercream too soft. This recipe can be halved if needed. Don't be put off anymore. Buttercream for everyone.

INGREDIENTS

100 g (3½ oz/½ cup) Copha or vegetable shortening, softened to room temperature

250 g (9 oz/1 cup) butter

1 teaspoon vanilla

500 g (1 lb 2 oz/4 cups) icing (confectioners') sugar

pinch of salt

Combine the Copha and butter in the bowl of a freestanding electric mixer fitted with the paddle attachment (we don't recommend doing this by hand). Beat on medium speed for 2–3 minutes until super light and fluffy.

Reduce the speed to low and add the vanilla. Gradually add the icing sugar and salt. Beat until well combined and fluffy. If you're going to use your buttercream on the same day, don't refrigerate it as it will get too hard. Feel free to refrigerate any leftover buttercream.

Mayonnaise

Makes approx. 250 ml (8½ fl oz/1 cup)

We gave you aioli in our first book, and now we give you mayo: the one sauce we go through the most at the Deli. You people love your creamy mayo-based sauces, and you like them on everything! My goodness, the amount of mayo we use in our sandwiches alone is enough to make you not want to eat them … wait a second, what am I saying? You love it because of the amount of mayo. Today's your day; you get to make your own. And surprisingly, our mayo uses ingredients most people have in their cupboards. Though this might mean our grocery sales go down, we encourage you to make your own mayo and see that it's a fraction of the price of the ready-made stuff. Double this recipe and ready yourself for the apocalypse. Added bonuses: there are no raw eggs; it's safe for pregnant people; it lasts for ages; and it's super yum.

Use this mayonnaise in Russian Dressing (page 202), Creamy Pesto Potato (page 041), Ze German Potato (page 043) and Sushi Salad (page 050).

INGREDIENTS

115 g (4 oz/½ cup) silken tofu

½ teaspoon salt

½ teaspoon black salt

1 teaspoon caster (superfine) sugar

60 ml (4 fl oz/¼ cup) unsweetened soy milk

2 teaspoons apple-cider vinegar

2 teaspoons dijon mustard

250 ml (8½ fl oz/1 cup) vegetable oil

Combine all the ingredients, except the oil, in a blender and blend until combined.

With the motor still running on medium speed, slowly drizzle in the oil.

If you prefer a thinner mayo (i.e. for a salad dressing), add a little hot water, with the blender running, after the oil has been added.

LITERALLY NO NEED TO BUY EGG MAYO ANYMORE. SHANNON'S NAILED IT.

Pesto

Makes approx. 250 ml (8½ fl oz/1 cup)

Because basil can be quite expensive, buy heaps and heaps of it in summer when it's cheap and far superior in quality. We suggest buying a couple of bunches to make big batches of pesto to freeze in resealable plastic bags.

Pesto has a million uses, but here are a few ideas: layer it on your Pizza Base (page 186), use it on Scrolls (page 185), in Lasagne (page 105), with Mayonnaise (opposite), Creamy Pesto Potato Salad (page 041) or, when you're feeling lazy but still want home-cooked spaghetti, toss some pesto through with lemon and olive oil … OK, now you come up with some ideas.

Also, before you throw away any leftover herbs or greens while cooking, or your wilting herbs or greens give up the fight, turn them into pesto. Parsley, rocket, spinach, kale (blanched), broccoli (cooked) – turn them all into pesto!

INGREDIENTS

approx. 200 g (7 oz/4 cups, firmly packed) basil leaves (approx. 1 bunch)

125 ml (4 fl oz/½ cup) extra-virgin olive oil

40 g (1½ oz/¼ cup) pine nuts, or pepitas (pumpkin seeds) for a nut-free option, toasted in a dry pan

25 g (1 oz/¼ cup) parmesan

1 garlic clove

1 teaspoon salt

Chuck all the ingredients in a regular or high-speed blender and blend until smooth. Be careful not to over-blend or you will heat the basil.

Russian Dressing

Makes 500 ml (17 fl oz/2 cups)

I want to meet the person who thought it was a good idea to mix all the sauces together. It was probably a three-year-old, 'cause that's what you do when you're three. Or just one lazy person who did away with having four jars and put it all into one instead. Genius. No, I know there's a whole story behind the creation of Russian dressing but, really, what a genius. Hysterical that some of the best sauces of the Western world – Russian, Thousand Island, McDonald's Special Sauce – are all just combos of the crappy, bad-for-you, sugary sauces masked by a fancy name.
Look, we don't care, we don't judge; we just know that it works. It's a true revelation.
All condiments in one place, making sweet, saucy love all over your burgers and Reubens and potato salads. May we never want for another sauce again.

INGREDIENTS

500 g (1 lb 2 oz/2 cups) Mayonnaise (page 200)

60 g (2 oz/¼ cup) gherkin relish

60 g (2 oz) ketchup

60 g (2 oz) dijon mustard

1 teaspoon onion powder

Mix all the ingredients together and store in the fridge for a long, long time.

MAYONNAISE

RUSSIAN DRESSING

PESTO

SATAY SAUCE

Satay Sauce

Makes approx. 750 ml (25½ fl oz/3 cups)

Like peanut butter, you would struggle to find someone who would refuse peanut sauce when offered. This is Shannon's super yum, but not super traditional, satay sauce. We use this recipe on our version of a Banh mi tofu roll, which we call the 'Anaphylaxis of Evil' (a combo of this satay sauce, pickled chilli paste, salt and pepper tofu, shredded pickled carrot, bean sprouts, cucumber and coriander). It's really, really good. Coat some tofu or chicken in the sauce, skewer it and you have a party on your hands. Like all the other sauces, it's a good idea to keep a jar of this in the fridge for a spontaneous stir-fry or for late-night snacking with some roti bread.

INGREDIENTS

1 tablespoon coconut oil or vegetable oil

1 tablespoon grated ginger

1 large garlic clove, minced

1 tablespoon chilli paste

250 ml (8½ fl oz/1 cup) coconut milk

125 ml (4 fl oz/½ cup) water

1 tablespoon brown or palm sugar

60 ml (2 fl oz/¼ cup) light soy sauce

125 g (4½ oz/½ cup) chunky peanut butter

80 ml (2½ fl oz/⅓ cup) lime juice

1 tablespoon sesame oil

3 tablespoons fish sauce

S&P

Heat the coconut oil in a large frying pan over a medium heat and gently fry the ginger and garlic for 1 minute. Add the remaining ingredients and simmer over a low heat for 5 minutes. Check and adjust the seasoning if necessary. This sauce will last for weeks in an airtight jar or container in the fridge.

ALSO PUT ON EVERYTHING.

PORTION THIS SAUCE AND
FREEZE IN RESEALABLE PLASTIC
BAGS SO WHEN THE TIME IS
RIGHT YOU HAVE EXACTLY WHAT
YOU NEED ON HAND.

Red Sauce

Makes approx. 2 kg (4 lb 6 oz)

IF YOU HAVE ONE SAUCE ON HAND AT ALL TIMES, MAKE IT THIS ONE. This should be as normal as having salt and pepper in your pantry. With red sauce comes all possibilities, from the laziest of uses (pasta and sauce) to the most decadent and extravagant (paella, savoury pies, lasagne). Red sauce is the base of (most) all delicious meals. Please think of how easy your life would be if you had batches of this in the freezer. Think soup, pizza, pasta, soffrito – everything. Your effort now will be rewarded with relief by your future, exhausted, can't-be-bothered self for many, many nights ahead.

INGREDIENTS

125 ml (4 fl oz/½ cup) extra-virgin olive oil

2 large brown onions, roughly chopped

6 large garlic cloves, roughly chopped

½ fennel bulb, roughly chopped

½–1 teaspoon chilli flakes

1 teaspoon salt, plus a big pinch

1 kg (2 lb 3 oz) ripe tomatoes, cored, blanched and peeled

1 x 700 g (1 lb 9 oz) bottle passata (puréed tomatoes)

1 teaspoon dried oregano

½ teaspoon pepper

1 bay leaf

250 ml (8½ fl oz/1 cup) water

½ bunch of fresh basil, leaves picked

Heat the oil in a large frying pan over a medium heat and fry the onion, garlic and fennel with the chilli flakes and a big pinch of salt. Once softened, add all the remaining ingredients except the water and basil.

Pour the water into the empty passata bottle, give it a shake and pour into the sauce. Bring to the boil, then simmer over a low heat for anywhere up to 3 hours, but a minimum of 1 hour. If it seems like it's drying out, add a splash of water. At the end of the cooking time, add the fresh basil.

Remove the bay leaf and use a hand-held blender to blend the sauce until smooth. Check and adjust the seasoning if necessary.

Veg Stock

Makes approx. 1.5 litres (51 fl oz/6 cups)

To keep an excess of veg stock in your fridge or freezer is the most admirable and impressive thing you could do in the kitchen. To be able to whip out that cup of home-made stock for a recipe and not have to rely on reconstituting a bouillon cube, you're a hero to yourself and the world. Making it is a lengthy but totally worthwhile process with many future benefits. Here's the best bit: veg stock uses up all the veg. Keep a big resealable plastic bag in the freezer and fill it with onion skins, carrot peels, stalks, any leftover veg from a recipe. Treat it like a compost bin for your freezer; just leave out the mouldy bits. Your stock will thank you.

INGREDIENTS

2 carrots, roughly chopped

1 parsnip, peeled and roughly chopped

2 large brown onions, quartered

1 garlic head, halved through the middle

1 leek end, washed VERY well

1 fennel bulb including top, cut into 6 pieces

80 ml (2½ fl oz/⅓ cup) extra-virgin olive oil, plus extra for frying

½ bunch of celery, chopped and washed

handful of dried mushrooms

1 tomato, skin on and quartered

2 bay leaves

1 rosemary sprig

½ lemon, sliced

¼ bunch of thyme

½ bunch of dill, stalks only

½ bunch of flat-leaf (Italian) parsley, roughly chopped

1 tablespoon black peppercorns

3 green cardamom pods, bruised with the side of a knife

250 ml (8½ fl oz/1 cup) white wine

S&P

Preheat the oven to 180–200°C (350–400°F).

Put the carrot, parsnip, onion, garlic, leek and fennel in a roasting tin, drizzle with the oil and scatter over some salt. Roast until golden.

Heat the largest stockpot you have over a medium heat, add a little oil and fry the remaining ingredients, except the wine, until soft, then mix in the roasted veg.

Deglaze the roasting pan with the wine, stir to remove any bits stuck to the bottom, then add the wine to the stockpot. Cover the vegetables with water and bring to the boil. Reduce the heat to a gentle simmer, cover with a lid, left slightly ajar, and simmer for 2 hours. Check and adjust the seasoning if necessary, then strain into one large airtight container or several smaller containers or resealable plastic bags, discarding the solids. By portioning your stock into multiple containers or bags, you'll have what you need for multiple meals ready to go.

FRIENDS, THERE'S A WORLD OF DIFFERENCE BETWEEN HOMEMADE STOCK AND A CUBE.

Caramel Sauce

Makes approx. 500 ml (17 fl oz/2 cups)

Caramel sauce. Do it. For all your sweet needs.
Yes, there's sour cream in this. As you know, Shannon isn't satisfied with 'good enough for vegans'; this caramel sauce has to stand up next to its dairy cousin. Because traditional caramels use thick cream, the best substitute is vegan sour cream. And as far as golden syrup goes, if you're in a country that doesn't have it, look up the best equivalent ingredient. Very important.

INGREDIENTS

180 g (6½ oz) butter

125 g (4½ oz) light brown sugar

125 g (4½ oz) caster (superfine) sugar

125 g (4½ oz) golden syrup

50 g (1¾ oz) sour cream

½–1 teaspoon good-quality salt

Melt the butter, sugars and golden syrup in a small saucepan over a medium heat. Bring to the boil and cook for about 3 minutes, then add the sour cream and salt. Whisk well to combine, then boil gently for another minute, or until thickened.

Leave to cool until thick, then drizzle over EVERYTHING.

Note: This sauce can be stored in the fridge for ages and reheated when needed.

Chocolate Sauce

Makes 185 ml (6 fl oz/¾ cup)

This is actually the vegan version of Ice Magic/Magic Shell; the minute it hits something cold, it goes solid. This sauce is great for drizzling on cakes, ice cream, milkshakes, everything. And you really should put it on everything, so don't hold back.

It's important to note the use of refined coconut oil in this recipe. This achieves the perfect chocolate sauce without actually tasting like coconut. Lots and lots of vegan sweets taste like they are made with or based on coconut, and that's simply the extra-virgin coconut oil at work. Power to you if that's your vibe. Go ahead and use the extra-virgin, but we want our chocolate sauce to taste only like chocolate sauce, which is why we prefer the refined stuff.

INGREDIENTS

150 g (5½ oz) dark chocolate chips (white chocolate is not interchangeable in this recipe)

1 tablespoon refined coconut oil

good pinch of salt (we like it hefty, but it depends how salty you want it; leave it out altogether if you don't like salty chocolate)

Combine the chocolate and coconut oil in a heatproof bowl and microwave on high for 1 minute. Stir, then heat again, in 10-second increments, stirring until smooth and well combined. Check after each time; the chocolate should look almost melted, but not completely melted. If you do not have a microwave, melt the chocolate in the top of a double boiler over a saucepan of simmering water. Mix in the salt.

Use this chocolate sauce on the Banana Split Cake (page 161), any of the frappés or milkshakes in the Drinks chapter (page 213) but, in particular: Lenny's Peanut Butter Dream (page 222), Choc Hazelnut Excess Frappé (page 218) and the Salty Caramel Pretzel Shake (page 221).

Note: Store in the fridge in a sealed jar. It may become solid and hard, so just heat it in the microwave or put the jar in a pot of boiling water to melt.

IMPORTANT LESSON:

USING REFINED COCONUT OIL SAVES YOU FROM EVERYTHING TASTING LIKE COCONUT.

TASTY DRINKS

We sell way, way more drinks beyond basic teas and coffees than any food deli should. And it's all because of one very special Jacqui, once a long-standing customer, now an important piece of the Deli puzzle and orchestrator of our drinks program. She came to the Deli like a force of nature, more excited about drinks than anything else. Well, maybe not anything else; she really loves *Twin Peaks* and dogs and *RuPaul's Drag Race* and, well, lots of things, and she has incorporated many of them into our weekly drink specials. It should be noted that Jacqui's ultimate love is making people happy. And her best tool? Sugar.

It was really hard to choose what drinks to include in this chapter, as our crazy list of shakes, frappés, hot chocolates and coffees have exploded since Jacqui's arrival. And, you guessed it, they're all equally popular. Here, she has curated a handful of her favourites. We've just added in a couple of refreshers to round out Jacqui's sweet tooth. And please, by all means, add some booze where it suits. We don't have a liquor licence at the Deli, but you better believe that at-home users are encouraged to make these drinks as saucy as possible.

Laura Palmer
(Cherry Pie Lemonade Iced Tea)

Makes approx. 2 litres (68 fl oz/8 cups)

An iced tea–lemonade hybrid with a *Twin Peaks* theme. The perfect refreshment for those hot days, with the addition of spiced cherry syrup. We think it would do Norma's Double R Diner cherry pie justice.

4 black tea bags or the equivalent amount of loose tea, if you prefer

925 ml (31½ fl oz) boiling water

925 ml (31½ fl oz) American-style lemonade

Cherry Syrup

400 g (14 oz/2 cups) jarred sour cherries, drained

230 g (8 oz/1 cup) caster (superfine) sugar

2 cinnamon sticks

1 star anise

5 whole black peppercorns

Brew the black tea in the water and leave to steep and cool for 4 hours.

Strain the tea through a piece of muslin (cheesecloth) to remove any sediment.

While the tea is brewing, make your cherry syrup. Mix all the ingredients in a saucepan and bring to the boil. Reduce the heat and simmer, stirring until the sugar has dissolved. Remove from the heat and leave to cool, then strain the syrup through a fine-mesh sieve. Discard the solids.

Mix the lemonade and 165 ml (5½ fl oz) cherry syrup into the tea. Store the remaining cherry syrup in the fridge for up to 1 month in a sterilised glass jar or bottle (see page 190) and use for any of your cherry syrup needs: over ice cream, as a cordial, in milkshakes, etc.

Photo page 217.

Jamaica Tea
(Hibiscus Iced Tea)

Makes 1 litre (34 fl oz/4 cups)

I feel sorry for people who haven't experienced the joy of drinking my favourite beverage: a tall, icy glass of Jamaica (ha-my-kah) tea. In Mexico, this delicious hibiscus flower–based tea is a standard agua fresca, always running in the drinks coolers alongside horchata and something with tamarind or watermelon. Don't be scared of flowers, friends. Also, don't be afraid to mix in your favourite spirit for a sassier version.

20 g (¾ oz/½ cup) dried hibiscus flowers

2 tablespoons–55 g (2 oz/¼ cup) caster (superfine) sugar (depending on how sweet you like your tea; start with 2 tablespoons and go from there)

1 cinnamon stick

3 whole cloves

1 litre (34 fl oz/4 cups) cold water

1 orange, cut into rounds, skin on

1 lemon, cut into rounds, skin on (optional)

Combine the flowers, sugar and spices with the water in a saucepan. Bring to the boil, then remove it from the heat and add the citrus. Leave to steep for 30 minutes.

Strain the tea through a fine-mesh sieve into a sterilised glass jar or bottle (see page 190). Allow to come to room temperature before refrigerating for up to 1 week.

Serve over plenty of ice with fresh orange and lemon slices, if using.

Photo page 216.

YOU CAN FIND HIBISCUS FLOWERS IN MOST LATIN OR MIDDLE EASTERN GROCERY STORES.

Raspberry Basil Lemonade

Makes 1 litre (34 fl oz/4 cups)

Raspberries and basil = BFF. Add some lemon and you've covered all the bases of sweet, savoury and sour. This drink is what summer dreams are made of. Just don your sunnies, get some SPF 30 and make a day of it. Nothing else need apply.

---

125 ml (4 fl oz/½ cup) lemon juice

1 lemon, cut into 8 wedges

115 g (4 oz/½ cup) caster (superfine) sugar

60 g (2 oz/½ cup) fresh or frozen raspberries

2 whole basil sprigs, including stalks

1 litre (34 fl oz/4 cups) water

ice cubes, to serve

Combine all the ingredients, except the water, in a jug or container and muddle everything together with a wooden muddler until well combined. Top with the water, stir well and refrigerate until ready to use. The flavours will develop even more with time.

Serve over plenty of ice and feel free to add the booze of your choice if that's your vibe.

Photo page 217.

Jalapeño Limeade

Makes 1 litre (34 fl oz/4 cups)

This drink is the perfect combo of both our personalities. Add tequila and you've got us all rounded out. Spicy, sweet, sour, smoky, bold … that's us. And while we wholeheartedly love this drink sans booze, this is a great one to assist in the pack down and clean up after shutting the doors on a Saturday after a long, long week and long, long queues of customers (thank you). Plus, this drink is awesome if you love the Jalapeño Margarita at Smith & Daughters.

---

1 lime, cut into 8 wedges

125 ml (4 fl oz/½ cup) lime juice (approx. 1 lime)

115 g (4 oz/½ cup) caster (superfine) sugar

¼–½ fresh jalapeño (seeds removed, depending on how spicy you want it)

1 litre (34 fl oz/4 cups) water

ice cubes, to serve

Combine the lime, lime juice, sugar and jalapeño in a jug or container and muddle everything together with a wooden muddler until well combined, releasing all the flavours and leaving lots of bits. Taste the mixture and check if it needs more heat (keep in mind, this isn't about how much of a wimp you are, it's about whether or not the jalapeños are spicy, as they vary in heat at different times of the year).

Add the water and give it a good mix, then store in the fridge.

Serve over ice in tall glasses and don't be afraid to add a cheeky shot of literally any spirit – though we prefer tequila or gin, always.

Photo page 217.

JALAPEÑO LIMEADE

CHOC CARAMEL
CORN FRAPPÉ

LAURA PALMER

RASPBERRY
BASIL
LEMONADE

Choc Hazelnut Excess Frappé

Serves 1

One of our most decadent, excessive shakes of all time. But what's the point if you're not going all out? You're ordering a shake, so make it worthwhile. The Choc Hazelnut Excess ran as a special for one week only, but we still get requests for it all the time. It's rich but by no means sickly, and the hazelnuts! Oh boy, the hazelnuts! Let's just say it tastes exactly like a liquid Ferrero Rocher and leave it right there.

---

2 scoops vanilla ice cream (your favourite)

70 g (2½ oz) whole hazelnut chocolate (we use Vego bars at the Deli – not only do they contain whole hazelnuts, but the chocolate is blended with a hazelnut paste. It's heaven in a chocolate bar! If you can't find it, blend whole hazelnuts and chocolate together instead.)

100 ml (3½ fl oz) non-dairy milk of your choice

½ tablespoon choc hazelnut spread of your choice

2 pinches of salt

handful of ice cubes, for blending

whipped cream, to garnish

hazelnuts, crushed (optional)

Combine all the ingredients, except the ice, in a blender and blitz until combined. Add a handful of ice cubes and blend until smooth.

Pour into a glass and top with whipped cream. You can also dust with chocolate powder or garnish with any extra chocolate, or crushed hazelnuts if you've got them.

Photo page 216.

Choc Caramel Corn Frappé
(Garmonbozia)

Serves 1

Jacqui, our resident *Twin Peaks* freak was entrusted with the task of coming up with weekly *Twin Peaks*–themed drinks in the lead-up and for the duration of Lynch's revival episodes. Needless to say, she had a damn fine time.

This was one of Jacqui's favourite drinks from the *Twin Peaks* specials. In Jacqui's words, 'Garmonbozia, in the Black Lodge, is presented in the form of creamed corn. How on earth could I use creamed corn in a drink and still keep it tasty? I'll tell you how – I couldn't! Chocolate and caramel corn, however, in a beautiful iced frappé? That's a winning combination.'

---

2 scoops vanilla ice cream (your favourite)

2 tablespoons chocolate powder

1½ tablespoons Caramel Sauce (page 210), plus extra to garnish

5 g (¼ oz/½ cup) caramel popcorn, plus extra to garnish

25 g (1 oz) honeycomb (optional; if you can get your hands on it)

pinch of salt

100 ml (3½ fl oz) non-dairy milk of your choice

2 handfuls of ice cubes, for blending

whipped cream, to garnish

Combine all the ingredients, except the ice, in a blender and pulse until smooth. Add the ice cubes and blend until thick and smooth, but don't over-blend!

Pour into a glass, top with whipped cream and garnish with some caramel sauce and/or caramel popcorn. Enjoy!

Photo page 217.

Eggnog

Makes 1 litre (34 fl oz/4 cups)

When the festive season hits, we have to indulge our customers in their favourite, not-readily-available holiday treats. One of those is giant milk bottles filled with our house-made eggnog. It flies off the shelves of the Deli. It's thick, spiced and most Aussies have no idea what the real deal is even meant to taste like. But let me tell you, it's like Christmas in a glass.

---

3 tablespoons custard powder

75 g (2¾ oz) caster (superfine) sugar

½ teaspoon ground cinnamon

½ teaspoon mixed spice

60 ml (2 fl oz/¼ cup) rum

1 litre (34 fl oz/4 cups) unsweetened soy milk (if you use sweetened or vanilla, you may have to reduce the sugar. Using unsweetened milk allows you to control the sweetness.)

½ teaspoon vanilla

¼ teaspoon salt

Combine the custard powder, sugar, spices and rum in a saucepan. Pour in 125 ml (4 fl oz/½ cup) soy milk and whisk to create a smooth paste. Slowly add the remaining soy milk and the vanilla and salt, whisking constantly.

Set the saucepan over a medium–low heat and whisk constantly until the custard thickens.

Pour into a jug and allow to come to room temperature before refrigerating. It will keep for about 1 week in the fridge.

Note: More often than not, custard powder is vegan. Just have a look at the label. And we haven't tried it 'cause we can't get it in Australia, but our American friends should try this recipe using pudding mix.

Photo page 159.

Coco Black

Serves 1

My absolute favourite way to consume coffee. It was the creation of a super talented former barista of ours, Milena, who just said, 'You know what would taste good … ' It's just SO refreshing. If you're anything like me, you'll take that caffeine in a hip flask or straight through an IV drip, but that's not socially acceptable. This way, you can literally drink coffee like water. Just to be clear, I don't fool myself into thinking that drinking coconut water with my coffee means I'm hydrated. I'm just in it for the tasty, refreshing caffeine.

---

250 ml (8½ fl oz/1 cup) coconut water

30 ml (1 fl oz) shot of espresso (at the Deli we use a double ristretto for a bit of extra oomph! It's also permissable and super yum to use cold-brew concentrate, or straight up cold brew. Keep in mind, if you're just using cold brew, you may want to increase the coffee and reduce the coconut water to make sure your caffeine needs are still met.)

ice cubes, to serve

Pour the coconut water into a glass filled with ice. Add the espresso and shake or stir to combine.

Consume all day, every day. Not just for summertime.

ADD AS MUCH RUM AS YOUR HOLIDAY SITUATION REQUIRES.

Mint Chip Shake

Serves 1

Chocolate and mint are a fresh, decadent match made in heaven. The only bummer about this shake is how easily consumed it is (aka gone in two seconds). It's just too nice.

---

2 scoops mint chip ice cream (your favourite)

100 ml (3½ fl oz) non-dairy milk of your choice

45 g (1½ oz/¼ cup) chocolate chips (optional, for the shake and garnish)

1–2 (or more) drops natural green food colouring (optional; use more or less, or none at all, depending on how green you want it)

handful of ice cubes, for blending

whipped cream, to garnish

mint leaves, to garnish (optional)

Combine all the ingredients, except the ice, in a blender and blitz until combined. Add the ice cubes and blend until smooth.

Pour into a glass and top with whipped cream. You can also garnish with extra chocolate chips. And if you want to be extra fancy (and literal), put a mint leaf on top.

Note: We say extra choc chips 'cause sometimes the mint chip ice cream just doesn't have enough chocolate. And we know you. You like your chocolate.

Salty Caramel Pretzel Shake

(James Hurley's Salty Tears)

Serves 1

At the end of the day, salty and sweet are meant to be together. Hence why this pretzel, caramel and chocolate number was always going to be a winner at the Deli. This shake is another *Twin Peaks* tribute from Jacqui. As she puts it, this is a decadent, salty-sweet treat to honour *Twin Peaks'* best loved emo, James Hurley. It's delicious and much nicer than drinking your own tears. Now get on your bike and go make this!

---

2 scoops ice cream (your favourite)

2½ tablespoons chocolate powder

1½ tablespoons Caramel Sauce (page 210), plus extra to garnish

80 g (2¾ oz/¾ cup) pretzels, plus extra to garnish

¼ teaspoon salt

100 ml (3½ fl oz) non-dairy milk of your choice

2 handfuls of ice cubes, for blending

whipped cream, to garnish

Combine all the ingredients, except the ice, in a blender and pulse until smooth. Add the ice cubes and blend until thick and smooth, but don't over-blend!

Pour into a glass, top with whipped cream and caramel sauce, and garnish with pretzels.

Lenny's Peanut Butter Dream

Serves 1

Because dogs are such an important part of the Deli, and because we love them and our customers love them, we would be remiss not to include a little recipe with a dog dedication. Jacqui, also a dog-lover and known to wear a badge reading 'dogs make me emotional', created this frappé as an ode to her standard poodle nephew, Lenny, who loooooves peanut butter. This is his drink. It's a thick, smooth, icy-cold treat – the perfect peanut buttery, chocolatey, salty number. Oh, and P.S., we love dogs AND frappés. Maybe equally. Maybe dogs more.

INGREDIENTS

2 scoops vanilla ice cream (your favourite)

2 tablespoons chocolate powder

1 tablespoon crunchy peanut butter

100 ml (3½ fl oz) non-dairy milk of your choice

4–5 ice cubes, for blending

whipped cream, to garnish

Combine the ice cream, chocolate powder, peanut butter and milk in a blender and blitz until combined. Add the ice cubes and pulse until smooth. The ice only slightly thickens the texture, but keeps your shake perfectly cool and refreshing.

Pour into a cup and top with copious amounts of whipped cream.

LENNY

Blue Heaven Shake

Serves 1

The eternal question: should 'blue' be something you consume? Does 'blue' exist in a natural form? It's perplexing to most and there's no clear history on why Blue Heaven is a flavour, why it only really exists in Victoria, Australia, and why no one can really describe it. It's pure sugary (evil) goodness. Some say vanilla, some say vanilla and raspberry. You may not be able to get your hands on this syrup anywhere in the world outside Victoria, but it's blue, it exists, people love it and it's on the cover of this book. Thank your lucky Blue Heavens.

INGREDIENTS

2 scoops vanilla ice cream (your favourite)

100 ml (3½ fl oz) non-dairy milk of your choice

60 ml (2 fl oz/¼ cup) Blue Heaven syrup

6–7 ice cubes, for blending

whipped cream, to garnish

Combine all the ingredients, except the ice, in a blender and blitz until combined. Add the ice cubes and blend until smooth.

Pour into a glass and top with whipped cream.

Index

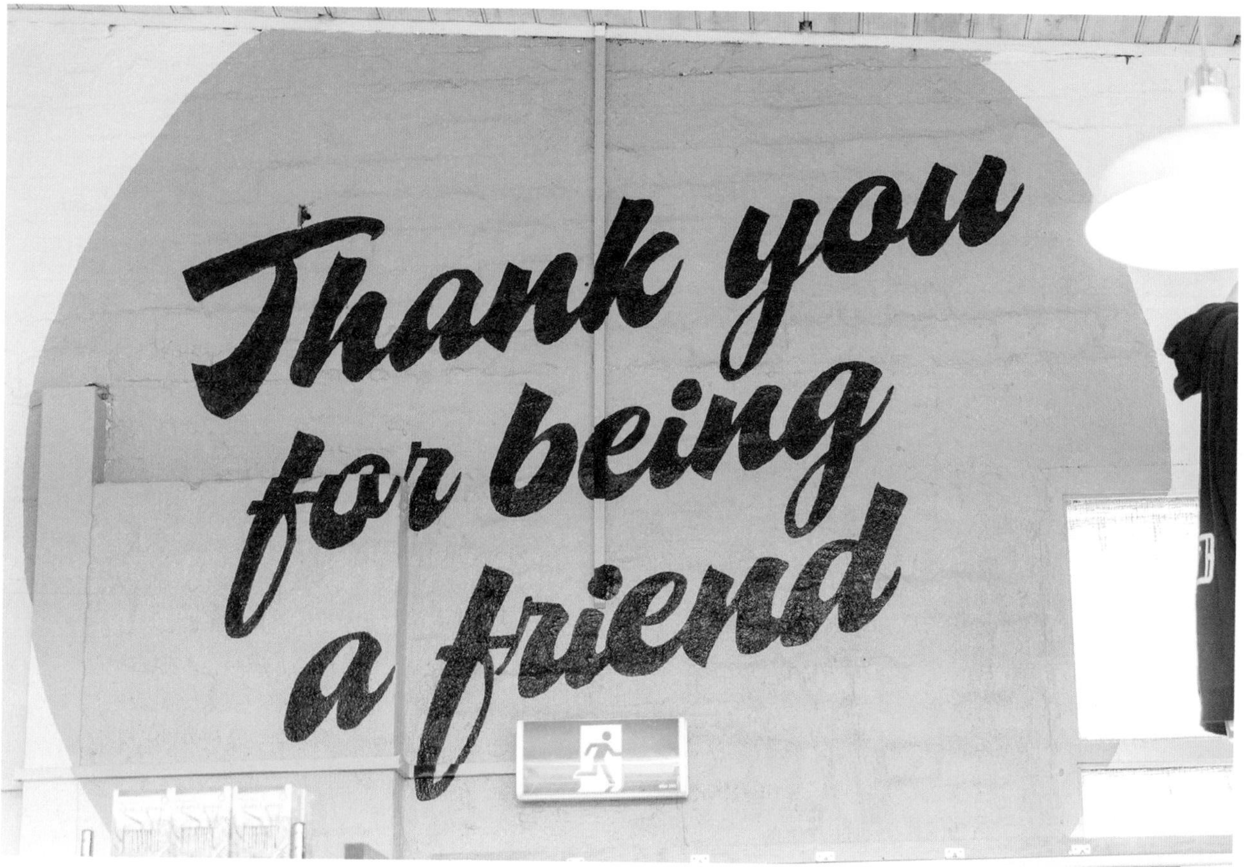
Thank you
for being
a friend

Thanks

SHANNON

Mum & Richard, Antoni & D, Jayden & Ness, Beccie, Noelie, Dad, Grandma, Puppy, Tamara, Deb, Mo & Callum. All my kitchen staff, who let me do things in my own 'special' way and put up with it. All my non-vegan chef friends, for letting me invade their kitchens to get vegan food out to the world. Special thanks to my hospo family: Duncan, Morgy, Moyle, Victor, Jerry, Eliza & Kimchi Pete for having my back and always encouraging me to push when others didn't.

MO

Callum, Shannon, Mom & Dad, Grams & Pops, Rae, Casey, Marilyn, Robert, Heath, Sarah, Charlotte & Ruby, Danielle, Matt, Stella & Ollie, Greg Bennick, Alice, Tyrone & Gus, Emillie & Lloyd, Charney, Tabby & EJ, Leslie Knope, Colette, Marina, Ashley, Danielle Corns, Bronwyn, Chris & Cassidy, Hannah, Steven, Lily Jane & Millie, Heather, Jason & Brandie Bailey, Patsy, Hayley & Sarah, Beth Gould. And all the people who supported this wild adventure, and this wild lady, and everyone else doing the good stuff and keeping positive.

SHANNON & MO

Our Deli crew, current and past. Thanks for shaping us into the place we are now, and into the even bigger places we will go!

Special thanks to our managers, without whom we couldn't expand this empire, write books and do more exciting things. Thank you.

Our HG Team, especially:

Jane Willson
Loran McDougall
Andrea O'Connor
Vaughan Mossop
Bonnie Savage
Deb Kaloper.

Designer, Builder, Fixer, Photographer, Everyman: Callum Preston.

Hair: Sam Castoro @RocketQueenStudios.

Makeup & Hair: Hannah Marshall.

Photography: Benn Wood, Bonnie Savage, Nicole Goodwin.

Our customers.

Our friends.

Our Deli community (dogs included).

This is for everyone who continues to support and believe in what we do and the greater goals we're trying to achieve.

IN LOVING MEMORY OF

AXL

About the authors

MO WYSE is a Seattle and New York expat. She studied journalism and has a background in production and events management, but dedicated her passion for creative, plant-based food to creating Smith & Daughters and Smith & Deli, two incredibly successful Fitzroy food businesses, where she is the logistical, front of house and marketing brain behind the gun team with Shannon Martinez. With a lifetime of hospitality under her belt, Mo understands the crucial inner workings of the front of house. The key to memorable, successful experiences in the hospitality industry – according to the S&D formula – is creating the perfect storm: brilliant, creative food, great service, strong branding and a reason to come back. The S&Ds consistently operate and generate that and more.

In terms of business development, Mo continues to support her front of house staff at both locations, as well as source new innovations for their businesses. Self-funded, self-taught and self-supported, Mo and Shannon thrive on their knowledge of what works and what doesn't. The fundamentals of the S&D brand are positivity, growth and a true dedication to excellence, both in service style and exciting, delicious food. Think products you can't get anywhere else, and at a level of quality not offered anywhere else. Seems simple, but that's what keeps people coming back.

Since the opening of both establishments and the release of *Smith & Daughters: A Cookbook (That Happens to be Vegan)*, Mo has been a guest speaker at numerous industry-relevant events, namely Restaurant Leaders Summit, LaTrobe University, Creative Mornings, General Assembly and more. Mo continues to focus on developing different expansion methods for the ever-growing S&D enterprise.

SHANNON MARTINEZ is an unlikely candidate to be the poster girl for plant-based dining. But she is and she's unstoppable. This time, it's coming from a different perspective. Being a meat eater gives this mega-talented chef the capability to create unique tastes and textures, unlike anything on the market today: ones that truly replicate meats, cheeses and good old family recipes. Shannon's mission to change the way the world perceives plant-based dining is most certainly underway. Meat eating, paired with a lifetime of cooking experience (literally since she can remember), outside-the-box methods and the willpower of a freight train, she will stop at nothing to perfect her recipes until they meet her own extremely high standards.

Armed with a strong hospitality network, and proven tenure in her industry with great success in plant-based dining, Shannon's talents are taken seriously in some of Australia's most meat-driven kitchens and among some of Australia's most unconvinced carnivorous chefs. Shannon's converted them, taken over their restaurants, sold out their seats and shown them just how mental the market for veg food is. It has worked every time. Shannon's latest goal is to make more interesting television, focusing on the many under-represented elements: females, good vegan food, music and entertainment.

Shannon has been cooking in Melbourne kitchens for the past twenty years; co-owns Australia's two most prolific plant-based businesses, Smith & Daughters and Smith & Deli; is co-author of *Smith & Daughters: A Cookbook (That Happens to be Vegan)*, and has been featured in all major Australian print media. Shannon has worked on the nation's biggest food events, has produced events with VICE House of Munchies, worked with Matty Matheson for BBQ festivals (vegan, of course) and done multiple restaurant takeovers, namely Belles Hot Chicken with Morgan McGlone. Needless to say, she is persistent and, truly, the sky may not be the limit. Stay tuned.

Published in 2018 by Hardie Grant Books, an imprint of Hardie Grant Publishing

Hardie Grant Books (Melbourne)
Building 1, 658 Church Street
Richmond, Victoria 3121

Hardie Grant Books (London)
5th & 6th Floors
52–54 Southwark Street
London SE1 1UN

hardiegrantbooks.com

 A catalogue record for this book is available from the National Library of Australia

Smith & Deli-cious
ISBN 978 1 74379 367 1

10 9 8 7 6 5 4 3 2 1

Publishing Director: Jane Willson
Managing Editor: Marg Bowman
Project Editor: Loran McDougall
Editor: Andrea O'Connor
Design Manager: Jessica Lowe
Designer: Vaughan Mossop
Food and on-site photographer: Bonnie Savage
Additional on-site photographer: Nicole Goodwin
Portrait and dog photographer: Benn Wood
Stylist: Deb Kaloper
Production Manager: Todd Rechner

Colour reproduction by Splitting Image Colour Studio
Printed in China by Leo Paper Product. LTD